Arduino for Kids

A cool guide to help kids develop robots and electronics

Priya Kuber
Rishi Gaurav Bhatnagar
Vijay Varada

BIRMINGHAM - MUMBAI

Arduino for Kids

First published: March 2017

Production reference: 1210317

Published by Packt Publishing Ltd.
Livery Place
35 Livery Street
Birmingham
B3 2PB, UK.

ISBN 978-1-78588-481-8

www.packtpub.com

Credits

Authors

Priya Kuber
Rishi Gaurav Bhatnagar
Vijay Varada

Reviewers

Avik Dhupar
Rubén Oliva Ramos

Commissioning Editor

Veena Pagare

Acquisition Editor

Tushar Gupta

Content Development Editor

Manthan Raja

Technical Editor

Danish Shaikh

Copy Editor

Manisha Sinha

Project Coordinator

Nidhi Joshi

Proofreader

Safis Editing

Indexer

Tejal Daruwale Soni

Graphics

Tania Dutta

Production Coordinator

Aparna Bhagat

Foreword

Willy Wonka was whom I wanted to be when I grew up, everything about him appealed to me - here you had a grown up who was tinkering around in his own factory creating new inventions - what made it even better was that his inventions were candies. I learnt coding in school, I started living part of my Willy Wonka dream by creating games in C++, as I created more of these technological 'candies' I realized that all of them were trapped inside this box of a computer. I would imagine what if you could unleash this computer from this box and let it out in the open, what if it could be free and everything would be a computer. Around this time a friend introduced me to the Arduino and I couldn't believe this small inexpensive piece of circuitry - it was more like magical wizardry, you see I grew up in the 90s when the fastest computer I had ever seen was much slower than the cheapest smartphone you can buy today. But more than anything, with the Arduino my ideas wouldn't anymore be limited to the computer screen but they could reach out into the real world - this new reality opened a pandora's box of innovative ideas and possibilities, some of which have made their way to the market thanks to Arduino's easy accessibility. It's been more than a decade since I was introduced to the Arduino, but I still use it to this day whenever I start with a new idea, it has become my 'Chocolate Factory'.

- Dhairya Dand

Principal

oDD, a futurist factory and lab

During the early 2009s Lechal was just an idea, to help navigate the blind from one place to another. We wanted to use vibrations as a medium to guide the blind. The human cognition, esp in the blind is complex, and very different from sighted people. It took us more than 25/30 product iterations to Lechal where it is right now. I came from a background of design and electronics, and found nothing as simple and modular as Arduino-Lilypad back in those days: It all started with this schematic, and prototype.

Even till the later stages of development, Arduino was the first tool we used to take ideas beyond the whiteboard.

As a new spinoff, Even the work that we're doing with present Arduino as Team Graviky, we utlize Arduino to prototype our ideas, and iterate fast. Arduino not only works well during our prototyping, but serves as a good manufacturing benchmark when we custom design our capture units, used to capture pollution.

- Anirudh Sharma

MIT spinoff Graviky Labs Pvt. Ltd.

About the Authors

Priya Kuber, is the first Indian woman to set up an open hardware company in India. At the age of 24, she was the founding CEO of *Arduino India* with a mission to empower students with the knowledge and tools to bring their creative ideas to life. She discovered Arduino in the year 2009 and has since contributed at several levels, including documentation, maintaining their official, blog and teaching workshops in rapid prototyping using Arduino, all across India. She has also won several hackathons and has mentored several winning teams. She now lives in San Francisco and works full-time on creating secure and impactful wearable technology. She is also the recipient of Silicon Valley's prestigious *Rajeev Circle Fellowship* and has given talks all around the world including at *TEDx*.

Rishi Gaurav Bhatnagar is a creative technologist who likes to work at the intersection of design and technology. He is an Intel software innovator, Arduino maker fellow, a volunteer at Random Hacks Of Kindness, also Campus Diaries 25 under 25- Science & Tech. When he is not tinkering with technology and storytelling, he spends time building new modules for students that help fuel their curiosity and build their innovation muscle.

Vijay Varada is an artist, engineer, and entrepreneur whose motto is, *create positive change in the world through art, design and technology for sustainable and exponential development and progress*. He is the CEO, and cofounder of *Fracktal Works*, which is engaged with design and research in the field of additive manufacturing, rapid prototyping, and product design with its line of desktop and industrial 3D printers aimed at using the technology to empower the abilities of students, engineers, designers, and industries. Vijay actively contributes to open source hardware projects, particularly assistive technologies for the blind.

About the Reviewers

Avik Dhupar is a hardware hacker and technology designer. He has been making and breaking circuits and toys ever since he was a kid. He was introduced to Arduino at a pretty young age, which changed his course of interest in life. He went on to join the official Arduino team, building and promoting Arduino awareness in India.

Currently, he works at Inveno, where he is making an inclusive and easy robotics and IoT platform for kids to learn programming.

He has worked extensively with Arduino, Raspberry Pi, and several other single board computers. He also enjoys designing musical instruments, particularly in the Eurorack format.

I would like to thank Packt for giving me the opportunity to review this amazing book. I would also like to thank my parents, who constantly supported me during the review of this book and influenced me to make and break things.

Rubén Oliva Ramos is a computer systems engineer from Tecnologico de Leon Institute, with a master's degree in computer and electronic systems engineering, teleinformatics and networking specialization from University of Salle Bajio in Leon, Guanajuato Mexico. He has more than five years of experience in developing web applications to control and monitor devices connected with Arduino and Raspberry Pi using web frameworks and cloud services to build Internet of Things applications.

He is a mechatronics teacher at University of Salle Bajio and teaches students on the master's degree in design and engineering of mechatronics systems. He also works at Centro de Bachillerato Tecnologico Industrial 225 in Leon, Guanajuato Mexico, teaching electronics, robotics and control, automation, and microcontrollers at Mechatronics Technician Career. He has worked on consultant and developer projects in areas such as monitoring systems and datalogger data using technologies such as Android, iOS, Windows Phone, Visual Studio .NET, HTML5, PHP, CSS, Ajax, JavaScript, Angular, ASP .NET databases (SQlite, mongoDB, and MySQL), and web servers (Node.js and IIS).

Ruben has done hardware programming on Arduino, Raspberry Pi, Ethernet Shield, GPS, and GSM/GPRS, ESP8266, and control and monitor systems for data acquisition and programming. He has written the book titled *Internet of Things Programming with JavaScript, Packt*.

His current job involves monitoring, controlling, and acquisition of data with Arduino and Visual Basic .NET for Alfaomega Editor Group.

I want to thank God for helping me reviewing this book, to my wife, Mayte, and my sons, Ruben and Dario, for their support, to my parents, my brother and sister whom I love and to all my beautiful family.

www.PacktPub.com

For support files and downloads related to your book, please visit www.PacktPub.com.

Did you know that Packt offers eBook versions of every book published, with PDF and ePub files available? You can upgrade to the eBook version at www.PacktPub.com and as a print book customer, you are entitled to a discount on the eBook copy. Get in touch with us at service@packtpub.com for more details.

At www.PacktPub.com, you can also read a collection of free technical articles, sign up for a range of free newsletters and receive exclusive discounts and offers on Packt books and eBooks.

https://www.packtpub.com/mapt

Get the most in-demand software skills with Mapt. Mapt gives you full access to all Packt books and video courses, as well as industry-leading tools to help you plan your personal development and advance your career.

Why subscribe?

- Fully searchable across every book published by Packt
- Copy and paste, print, and bookmark content
- On demand and accessible via a web browser

Customer Feedback

Thanks for purchasing this Packt book. At Packt, quality is at the heart of our editorial process. To help us improve, please leave us an honest review on this book's Amazon page at `https://www.amazon.com/dp/1785884816/`.

If you'd like to join our team of regular reviewers, you can e-mail us at `customerreviews@packtpub.com`. We award our regular reviewers with free eBooks and videos in exchange for their valuable feedback. Help us be relentless in improving our products!

Table of Contents

Preface

It is well known that early childhood experiences shape adult life. Hobbies have now transitioned from simple Lego buildings to well researched knowledge building toolkits. Albert Einstein said, *If you can't explain to a six year old, you don't understand it yourself*. This book is the attempt of 3 self-taught professional hobbyist-inventors to use their experience, to teach complex electronics to a 9-12 year old. This book contains the combined teaching experience of approximately 300 workshops conducted by 3 of the authors separately.

Learning, is a process, but effective learning is a skill. In this book, we have started with the fundamentals of critical thinking that all professional engineers use and translated it, to the level of children. We have ensured that the learning curve is relatable and includes the fundamentals of developing the research mindset, that is required in today's career, irrespective of their life choices.

We also took care of increasing the complexity level of the projects to a level, just within the reach of kids. Irrespective of their technical level, adults can use this book to build projects and bond with their kids. The components used are simple and easy to find in any market.

The time taken to complete each project, has also been carefully crafted to last 1 day. The assumption is that you can have productive fun with your kids for several weekends. Each project has also been kept independent from the other, to give a sense of completion and tangible accomplishment to the kids.

This world will need more engineers, designers, astronauts, story tellers, and visionaries. We hope that this book is going to be the first step in their scientific and creative journeys.

What this book covers

Chapter 1, *The World Around Us*, is about explicitly drawing the attention of the reader to the systems and processes around us, encouraging the reader to take notes and observations. Children are inspired by everyday things more than an abstract concept. Every system is split into sensor-microcontroller-actuator.

Chapter 2, *Systems and Logic*, proceeds to teach the young readers how logic works. Starting from simple algorithms, it teaches the child to reach complex systems by first creating simple substitute systems. For example, to make an alarm, this chapter first teaches them to prototype using an LED. Then later teach them to add a button to disable the alarm, and as a challenge, would ask them to make a special combination lock in the activity.

Chapter 3, *Components and Connections*, is about the basics of electronics and building blocks of circuits. The child will also get introduced to basic sensors that are available off the shelf, also will learn the logic of the sensors, to enable them to create their own. They learn the concept of electricity, current, and voltages and understand that they can be manipulated.

Chapter 4, *The Magic Wand*, is about introducing Arduino as the 'brain' of a system and will teach students how to operate. It teaches a child to set up the Arduino with vibrant picture instructions. It will introduce them to a set process of thinking an execution when solving problems or working with projects. This chapter will also talk about open source, and open source hardware - will talk about how open source has revolutionized technology., giving them a non-selfish view about technology.

Chapter 5, *Hello world!*, is the beginning of integration of all the knowledge that the readers have accumulated and write their first program in Arduino and create a light sensitive organism.

Chapter 6, *Safety box*, begins with the series of projects. Every child likes to keep secrets and what better a first project than getting the child to make a small safety box that will ring an alarm if opened. The project further includes a button to stop the alarm, and further guides the child to set a secret key code to stop the alarm.

Chapter 7, *Make a friend*. is about teaching the child learning the importance of making a friend by using proximity sensor. When the child brings a friend near to his/her toy friend , the toy's smile lights up. The child's toy would be made using playdough, with the proximity sensor as a belt.

Chapter 8, *Save Energy*, aims to show the child the positive impact that a sensor-based smart system can have on the environment. The system uses a simple LDR (light dependent resistor) , an Arduino and an LED. This is to demonstrate a simple porchlight turning automatically off when it is daytime, thus saving energy.

Chapter 9, *High 5!*, creates a very gratifying High-5ing robot to celebrate the child's accomplishment so far through the book. It combines sensors and actuators and gives the child a comprehensive understanding of building autonomous systems. You build a robot that High 5s you when you are close!

Chapter 10, *Plant, Meet Arduino*, is a fun and a challenging activity where the child will make a plant more interactive. The child will build a system that can find out if the plant is thirsty and intimate human about it.

What you need for this book

The latest version of Arduino IDE for your computer.

Who this book is for

This book is for children aged 9 and up and their parents, who may or may not have a technical background. This book is tailored around the central idea of introducing electronics as a fun and a curiosity-inducing exercise. This book can act as a bonding exercise between parent and child over the weekend.

Conventions

In this book, you will find a number of text styles that distinguish between different kinds of information. Here are some examples of these styles and an explanation of their meaning.

Code words in text, database table names, folder names, filenames, file extensions, path names, dummy URLs, user input, and Twitter handles are shown as follows: "We can include other contexts through the use of the include directive."

A block of code is set as follows:

```
int pin = 13;
void setup() {
 // put your setup code here, to run once:
 pinMode(pin,OUTPUT);
}
void loop() {
 // put your main code here, to run repeatedly:
dot();dot();dot();
dash();dash();dash();
dot();dot();dot();
delay(3000);
}
```

New terms and important words are shown in bold. Words that you see on the screen, for example, in menus or dialog boxes, appear in the text like this: "Clicking the **Next** button moves you to the next screen."

Warnings or important notes appear in a box like this.

Tips and tricks appear like this.

Reader feedback

Feedback from our readers is always welcome. Let us know what you think about this book—what you liked or disliked. Reader feedback is important for us as it helps us develop titles that you will really get the most out of.

To send us general feedback, simply e-mail `feedback@packtpub.com`, and mention the book's title in the subject of your message.

If there is a topic that you have expertise in and you are interested in either writing or contributing to a book, see our author guide at `www.packtpub.com/authors`.

Customer support

Now that you are the proud owner of a Packt book, we have a number of things to help you to get the most from your purchase.

Downloading the example code

You can download the example code files for this book from your account at `http://www.packtpub.com`. If you purchased this book elsewhere, you can visit `http://www.packtpub.com/support`and register to have the files e-mailed directly to you.

You can download the code files by following these steps:

1. Log in or register to our website using your e-mail address and password.
2. Hover the mouse pointer on the **SUPPORT** tab at the top.

3. Click on **Code Downloads & Errata**.
4. Enter the name of the book in the **Search** box.
5. Select the book for which you're looking to download the code files.
6. Choose from the drop-down menu where you purchased this book from.
7. Click on **Code Download**.

You can also download the code files by clicking on the **Code Files** button on the book's webpage at the Packt Publishing website. This page can be accessed by entering the book's name in the **Search** box. Please note that you need to be logged in to your Packt account.

Once the file is downloaded, please make sure that you unzip or extract the folder using the latest version of:

- WinRAR / 7-Zip for Windows
- Zipeg / iZip / UnRarX for Mac
- 7-Zip / PeaZip for Linux

The code bundle for the book is also hosted on GitHub at `https://github.com/PacktPublishing/Arduino-for-Kids`. We also have other code bundles from our rich catalog of books and videos available at `https://github.com/PacktPublishing/`. Check them out!

Errata

Although we have taken every care to ensure the accuracy of our content, mistakes do happen. If you find a mistake in one of our books—maybe a mistake in the text or the code—we would be grateful if you could report this to us. By doing so, you can save other readers from frustration and help us improve subsequent versions of this book. If you find any errata, please report them by visiting `http://www.packtpub.com/submit-errata`, selecting your book, clicking on the Errata Submission Form link, and entering the details of your errata. Once your errata are verified, your submission will be accepted and the errata will be uploaded to our website or added to any list of existing errata under the Errata section of that title.

To view the previously submitted errata, go to `https://www.packtpub.com/books/content/support` and enter the name of the book in the search field. The required information will appear under the Errata section.

Piracy

Piracy of copyrighted material on the Internet is an ongoing problem across all media. At Packt, we take the protection of our copyright and licenses very seriously. If you come across any illegal copies of our works in any form on the Internet, please provide us with the location address or website name immediately so that we can pursue a remedy.

Please contact us at `copyright@packtpub.com` with a link to the suspected pirated material.

We appreciate your help in protecting our authors and our ability to bring you valuable content.

Questions

If you have a problem with any aspect of this book, you can contact us at `questions@packtpub.com`, and we will do our best to address the problem.

1
The World around Us

Things you will learn about in this chapter are as follows:

- How things around you work
- How to ask questions when you are learning something new
- How to carefully record your observations

Have you ever wondered how things around you seem to talk to each other? How does your garage door know when to open? How does your night-lamp know when to switch the light on and off? How does your computer connect to the Internet and download interesting videos?

All the problems in the world are solved by one word–invention.

The word **In-ven-tion** originates from the Latin word *Inventio*, which means *finding out*. Human beings are called intelligent as they are able to understand, communicate, and change their surroundings. People who make these changes are called *inventors*.

Since prehistoric times, inventors have held a great power over the rest of humanity. Imagine a world without fire! Humans would not have been able to defend themselves or cook food. Imagine a life without wheels, where humans had to carry heavy weight on their backs. Every inventor has had some positive contribution to the society. It is cool to be an inventor. Inventors are no less than superheroes.

However, becoming an inventor is not an easy task, but so wasn't humans visiting the moon! Every human has the ability to be curious, ask questions, understand, learn, team-up, and build a solution. All it takes is taking one step at a time, just like climbing a set of stairs. Always imagine your solution at the top of a flight of stairs, break down your problem into small questions, connect those questions to your existing knowledge base, learn more from your available resources–be it friends, books, elders or internet. Expand your knowledge in related fields, figure out your solution. Try to build your solution, if it works, there you go, you have an invention! If not, think harder, question more!

And you young makers are invention-superheroes! Isn't it cool?

Solving problems – the best way out

The first step to gaining these superpowers is to keep an observation–notebook. This observation notebook will be your companion throughout your journey towards a desired solution.

Now that you have your own **invention-notebook**, write a question. What fascinates you in your everyday life? There is an answer for everything it is a matter of asking the right question.

A good invention-notebook is filled in regularly, and superheroes don't not give up till they have solved the problem!

The internet is a great tool to solve problems–let's call it the helpful genie in the bottle. During the course of building things with me, you will need to rub this bottle a lot and call the genie!

Brace yourselves, young invention-superheroes, you and your genie are ready to embark upon this wonderful world of inventing solutions to problems!

Now that we agreed that you want to solve problems, how do we define or recognize a problem?

A problem is nothing but a solution with a LOT of gift wraps. It is an opportunity for you to increase your knowledge base. The more data you have in your knowledge base, the harder problems you can solve, and the better your solutions can be.

Problems can be observed by you, or reported to you by others. Understanding the problem is the first step. Some good questions to ask would be as follows:

- What is the end result I want?
- Does any solution currently exist to solve it? (Search the internet, use your genie!)
- Is the current solution the best way it can be solved?

When you get the answer to the last two questions as *NO*, you try to break down the problem into small blocks, just like you chew the food before swallowing.

Take a very simple example: if your younger brother has a problem understanding how your night lamp turns on and off with a switch, you start by making a note in your inventor's notebook:

What do you see in the lamp?

- You see a bulb at the center, a shade, and a tail-like wire plugged into a socket; you write it down.
- Then you see the small switch, which makes the bulb go on and off Note that down too in your notebook. Start asking yourself what is in that switch that makes this lamp go on and off and how can it be related to the socket? Ask an elder to pull the plug off–try the switch.
- Does the bulb go on and off? No? Note that down in your inventor's notebook.
- Ask the elder to plug in the wire again. Try the switch now? Yes! Make a note of that in your notebook too.
- What did you learn? The lamp works when it is plugged in, and it is controlled by a switch.
- What makes the lamp work? What comes out of the socket? Can you explain it?
- Ask your genie! (Answer on the last page)

The beauty of taking notes

Can you recall your last birthday party? How old did you turn? What color clothes were you wearing? How many friends came to your birthday party? What were they all wearing? Of course you can recall all that by looking into your photo-album!

What were you thinking when you opened your best friend's present? Could that thought be captured in camera? No! Do you want to base your future interactions with your best friend based on how special they made you feel on that day? Yes!

Human thoughts and memories are short-lived; they change with time and new experiences. As we discussed, solving a problem takes a lot of time because each question leads to more! It is tough to keep a tab on all the thoughts.

But if you write it down, it's yours forever, as it was in that moment! As clear as a photograph! **Clarity** of your last thought is very important when you are trying to invent something new as you are linking the information you already knew to newer information. It is a chain that keeps on increasing with experience.

Hence, your inventors-notebook is your best friend!

Let's conduct a simple experiment to test your newly acquired inventor-power! Adult supervision is needed. The requirements are: a lemon, a paper clip, and a copper wire.

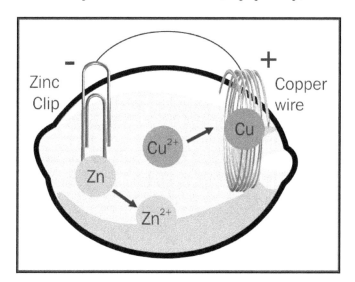

Procedure:

1. Request the adult to straighten the paper clip and cut about two inches of it and give you. Request the elder to remove the insulation from the household copper wire and cut two inches of it.
2. IN FRONT OF THE ADULT, try touching both the wires with your tongue (I know, it's not my favorite snack either!).
3. Now fix the two wires in the lemon in a way that they are as close as possible but DO NOT touch each other.
4. Now try licking the end of the wires.

Observation: Taste something tingly on your tongue?

Conclusion: Congratulations! You just 'tasted' electricity! Go brag to your friends!

 If you add one more lemon with similar paper clips and connect them, you can power an LED! Cool, eh?

⚠**Warning** *Cool as it may seem, electricity is a highly dangerous power, and you must ALWAYS have adult supervision while handling it. DO NOT ATTEMPT TO TASTE ANY ELECTRICITY THAT IS NOT COMING FROM the LEMON. This tingling sensation is magnified by several thousand times in real life, and all our appliances are built to withstand that kind of power; our human body is not, and imitating this stunt can be disastrous!*

What kind of questions have you noted in your inventors-notebook? Why is this happening? What will happen if you replace the copper wire with the same kind of paper clip instead? Write back to me at mail@priyakuber.in.

 Cool as it may seem, all the experiments in this book come with a warning sign: do not swallow the parts that we use to create a solution, and when in doubt, always call for an adult. Safety first!

The human body

Have you ever wondered how your body functions? Irrespective of your wonder, start making notes! Let me get you started with some basic questions.

Q1. If we were an advanced robot, how do we see?

Ans. Through the eyes (Duh!).

Q2. How do we hear?

Ans. Ears. (Don't chocolates and new toys sound great?)

Q3. How do we differentiate between touching a soft kitten from touching a stone?

Ans. Skin. (I know you prefer a soft kitten more than a stone, trust me, so do I!)

Our nose, ears, skin are all what we call sensors. (Remember, we are all advanced robots!)

And what happens when we touch something hot by mistake? We quickly withdraw our hands. Now a normal kid would not notice this, but you, as an invention-hero, would ask the right question–why does this happen?

Our skin, which is a sensor, senses the hot object and wants to protect itself from damage; it sends a signal to our brain through electrical pulses and returns with instructions on what to do–MOVE AWAY!

Our brain is a microcontroller. A microcontroller is what makes our bodies *intelligent*, and like any normal human being, a microcontroller is as intelligent as the amount of information that you store in it. (Think about the last time you did not study well for a test, were you able to answer the questions?)

A human body has millions of tiny sensors and has the most advanced processing controller–the brain!

Now how does your mom's cellphone know which friend of hers in calling?

She 'taught' the brain of the cellphone what name a number matched to.

So we reach our most important conclusion of the chapter–microcontrollers are only as intelligent as we make them.

Now here's an exercise for you:

Can you use the internet to find out what sensors can be used to replace human nose, ears, and skin to make a small cardboard robot that will sleep when you turn off the lights and keep the room quiet and stroke it gently? You will build it in due course of this book.

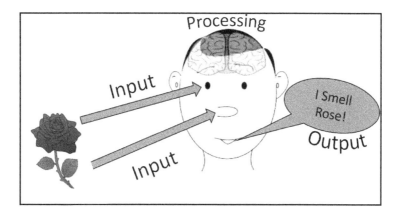

In the afore mentioned system, we see that all the inputs need to go to the brain to get instructions. The brain of this robot will be Arduino.

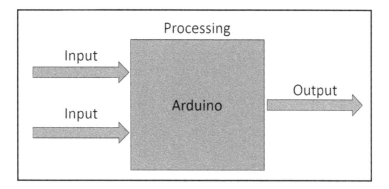

Stay tuned to find out more fun stuff!

Summary

In this chapter, you learnt that you are all inventing-superheroes. You learnt the importance of keeping an inventors-notebook. You learnt how to ask the right questions and to use Internet for solutions. You also learnt that a microcontroller is only as intelligent as you make it. You tasted the safest form of electricity and learnt a very important lesson **SAFETY FIRST** around anything that emits electricity.

2
Systems and Logic

Things you'll learn:

- What is a system
- What is code
- How does a code work
- What is the structure and various components of a code
- How to download, save and access a file in the Arduino IDE

What is a system?

Imagine system as a box which in which a process is completed. Every system is solving a larger problem, and can be broken down into smaller problems that can be solved and assembled. Sort of like a Lego set! Each small process has 'logic' as the backbone of the solution. Logic, can be expressed as an algorithm and implemented in code. As learnt in `Chapter 1`, *The World around Us* you can design a system to arrive at solutions to a problem.

Another advantage to breaking down a system into small processes is that in case your solution fails to work, you can easily spot the source of your problem, by checking if your individual processes work.

What is code?

Code is a simple set of written instructions, given to a specific program in a computer, to perform a desired task. Code is written in a computer language. As we all know by now, a computer is an intelligent, electronic device capable of solving logical problems with a given set of instructions.

Some examples of computer languages are Python, Ruby, C, C++ and so on.

 Find out some more examples of languages from the internet and write it down in your notebook.

What is an algorithm?

A logical set by step process, guided by the boundaries (or constraints) defined by a problem, followed to find a solution is called an algorithm. In a better and more pictorial form, it can be represented as follows:

$$\boxed{\text{Logic} + \text{Control} = \text{Algorithm}}$$

What does that even mean? Look at the following example to understand the process.

Let's understand what an algorithm means with the help of an example.

It's your friend's birthday and you have been invited for the party (Isn't this exciting already?). You decide to gift her something. Since it's a gift, let's wrap it. What would you do to wrap the gift? How would you do it?

- Look at the size of the gift
- Fetch the gift wrapping paper
- Fetch the scissors
- Fetch the tape
- Then you would proceed to place the gift inside the wrapping paper.
- You will start start folding the corners in a way that it efficiently covers the Gift.
- In the meanwhile, to make sure that your wrapping is tight, you would use a scotch tape.
- You keep working on the wrapper till the whole gift is covered (and mind you, neatly! you don't want mommy scolding you, right?).

What did you just do? You used a logical step by step process to solve a simple task given to you.

Again coming back to the sentence: *Logic + Control = Algorithm*

Logic here, is the set of instructions given to a computer to solve the problem. 'Control' are the words making sure that the computer understands all your boundaries.

Logic

Logic is the study of reasoning and when we add this to the control structures, they become algorithms.

Have you ever watered the plants using a water pipe or washed a car with it? How do you think it works?

The pipe guides the water from the water tap to the car. It makes sure optimum amount of water reaches the end of the pipe. A pipe is a control structure for water in this case. We will understand more about control structures in the next topic.

How does a control structure work?

Everything that we see around us, has a name. In a class, there are several students. When the teacher says *I will give the prize to the best student*. The student could be anyone in the class – Eric, Emily, Jonnathan, and so on.

We conclude, that the word student, is a variable.

Similarly, while starting to write code, we define a box, which can contain different values at different times, depending on the condition that we define. A control structure, defines the final value of the variables.

A precondition is the state of a variable before entering a control structure. In the gift wrapping example, the size of the gift determines the amount of gift wrapping paper you will use. Hence, it is a condition that you need to follow to successfully finish the task. In programming terms, such condition is called precondition. Similarly, a post condition is the state of the variable after exiting the control structure. And a variable, in code, is an alphabetic character, or a set of alphabetic characters, representing or storing a number, or a value. Some examples of variables are x, y, z, a, b, c, kitten, dog, robot

Let us analyze flow control by using traffic flow as a model. A vehicle is arriving at an intersection. Thus, the precondition is the vehicle is in motion. Suppose the traffic light at the intersection is red. The control structure must determine the proper course of action to assign to the vehicle.

Precondition: The vehicle is in motion.

Control Structure

Is the traffic light green? If so, then the vehicle may stay in motion.

Is the traffic light red? If so, then the vehicle must stop.

End of Control Structure

Postcondition: The vehicle comes to a stop.

Thus, upon exiting the control structure, the vehicle is stopped.

Thus, upon exiting the control structure, the vehicle is stopped.

If you wonder where you learnt to wrap the gift, you would know that you learnt it by observing other people doing a similar task through your eyes. Since our microcontroller does not have eyes, we need to teach it to have a logical thinking using code.

The series of logical steps that lead to a solution is called algorithm as we saw in the previous task. Hence, all the instructions we give to a micro controller are in the form of an algorithm. A good algorithm solves the problem in a fast and efficient way.

Blocks of small algorithms form larger algorithms. But algorithm is just code! What will happen when you try to add sensors to your code? A combination of electronics and code can be called a system.

$$sensors \rightarrow arduino \leftarrow code$$

Logic is universal. Just like there can be multiple ways to fold the wrapping paper, there can be multiple ways to solve a problem too!

A micro controller takes the instructions only in certain languages. The instructions then go to a compiler that translates the code that we have written to the machine.

What language does your Arduino Understand?

For Arduino, we will use the language processing. Quoting from `www.processing.org`, Processing is a flexible software sketchbook and a language for learning how to code within the context of the visual arts.

Processing is an **open source programming language** and **integrated development environment** (IDE). Processing was originally built for designers and it was extensively used in electronics arts and visual design communities with the sole purpose of teaching the fundamentals of computer sciences in a visual context. This also served as the foundations of electronic sketchbooks.

From the previous example of gift wrapping, you noticed that before you need to bring in the paper and other stationery needed, you had to see the size of the problem at hand (the gift).

What is a library?

In computer language, the stationery needed to complete your task, is called *Library*. A library is a collection of reusable code that a programmer can reuse instead of writing everything again.

Now imagine if you had to cut a tree, make paper, then color the paper into the beautiful wrapping paper that you used, when I asked you to wrap the gift. How tiresome would it be? (If you are inventing a new type of paper, sure, go ahead chop some wood!)

So before writing a program, you make sure that you have called all the right libraries.

 Can you search the internet and make a note of a few Arduino libraries in your inventor's diary?

Please remember, that libraries are also made up of code! As your next activity, we will together learn more about how a library is created.

Activity – Understanding the Morse Code

During the times before the two-way mobile communication, people used a one-way communication called the Morse code. The following image is the experimental setup of a Morse code. In 1836, Samuel Morse demonstrated the ability of a telegraph system to transmit information over wires. The information was sent as a series of electrical signals. Do not worry; we will not get into how you will perform it *physically*, but by this example, you will understand how your Arduino takes in instructions. We will show you the bigger picture first and then dissect it systematically so that you understand what a code contains.

The Morse code is made up of two components *short* and *long* signals. The signals could be electric form, like the way Samuel Morse did, or as a light pulse or sound. The following image shows how the Morse code looks like. A dot is a short signal and a dash is a long signal:

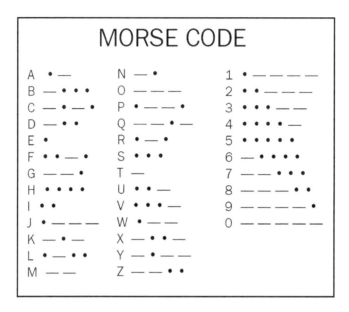

Interesting, right? Try encrypting your message for your friend with this dots and dashes. For example, **HELLO** would be:

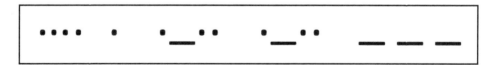

The image below shows how the Arduino code for Morse code will looks like.

```
int pin = 13;

void setup()
{
    pinMode(pin, OUTPUT);
}

void loop()
{
    dot(); dot(); dot();
    dash(); dash(); dash();
    dot(); dot(); dot();
    delay(3000);
}

void dot()
{
    digitalWrite(pin, HIGH);
    delay(250);
    digitalWrite(pin, LOW);
    delay(250);
}

void dash()
{
    digitalWrite(pin, HIGH);
    delay(1000);
    digitalWrite(pin, LOW);
    delay(250);
}
```

The piece of code in dots and dashes is the message SOS that I am sure you all know, is an urgent appeal for help.

SOS in Morse goes: dot dot dot; dash dash dash; dot dot dot.

Since this is a library, which is being created using dots and dashes, it is important that we define how the dot is read as a dot, and dash is read as a dash in the first place! The following sections will take smaller sections or pieces of main code and explain you how they work. As you follow along, we will also introduce some more interesting concepts.

What is a function?

Functions have instructions in a single line of code, telling the values in the bracket how to act. Let us see which one is the function in our code. Can you try to guess from the following screenshot?

```
void dot()
{
  digitalWrite(pin, HIGH);
  delay(250);
  digitalWrite(pin, LOW);
  delay(250);
}

void dash()
{
  digitalWrite(pin, HIGH);
  delay(1000);
  digitalWrite(pin, LOW);
  delay(250);
}
```

No? Let me help you! `digitalWrite()` in the preceding code is a function, that as you understand, writes on the correct pin of the Arduino.

`delay` is a function that tells the controller how frequently it should send the message. The higher the delay number, the slower will be the message (Imagine it as a way to slow down your friend who speaks too fast, helping you to understand him better!)

 Look up the internet to find out what is the maximum number that you stuff into delay.

What is a constant?

A constant is an just like a variable but with pre-defined, non-changeable values. What is an identifier you ask? An identifier is a name that labels the identity of a unique object or value.

As you can see from the above piece of code, HIGH and LOW are **Constants.**

Q: What is the opposite of **Constant**? **Ans: Variable**

The above food for thought brings us to the next section.

What is a variable?

As we discussed before, a variable is used to store a piece of information temporarily. The value of a variable changes, if any action is taken on it for example; Add, subtract, multiply, and so on.

A variable is used to store a piece of information temporarily. The value of a variable changes, if any action is taken on it for example; Add, subtract, multiply etc. (Imagine how your teacher praises you when you complete your assignment on time and scolds you when you do not!)

What is a datatype?

Datatypes are sets of data that have a pre-defined value. A real life example, could be a person's name – It is usually a word like Eric whereas the answer to the question *How much do you weigh?* would be a number like 95lbs. One can perform addition or subtraction on weight, but one cannot add or subtract someone's name! We come to the following conclusion:

- The datatype of name is a fixed value consisting of a word.
- The datatype of weight is a fixed value consisting of numbers.
- While writing code, we have the datatypes like integer, float, string, and so on.

Now look at the first block of the example program in the following screenshot:

```
int pin = 13;

void setup()
{
    pinMode(pin, OUTPUT);
}

void loop()
{
    dot(); dot(); dot();
    dash(); dash(); dash();
    dot(); dot(); dot();
    delay(3000);
}
```

int as shown in the above screenshot, is a **Datatype**.

The following table shows some of the examples of a datatype.

Datatype	Use	Example
int	describes an integer number is used to represent whole numbers	1, 2, 13, 99 and so on
float	used to represent that the numbers are decimal	0.66, 1.73 and so on
char	represents any character. Strings are written in single quotes	'A', 65 and so on
str	represent string	This is a good day!

With the above definition, can we recognize what pinMode is?

 Every time you have a doubt in a command or you want to learn more about it, you can always look it up at Arduino website. You could do the same for digitalWrite() as well!

From the `pinMode` page of `Arduino.cc` we can define it as a command that configures the specified pin to behave either as an input or an output.

Now that we understood datatypes, we can proceed to learn about using them with control structures.

Application of the control structure

We have already seen the working of a control structure. In this section, we will be more specific to our code. Now I draw your attention towards this specific block from the main preceding example:

```
void setup()
{
    pinMode(pin, OUTPUT);
}

void loop()
{
```

Do you see `void setup()` followed by a code in the brackets? Similarly `void loop()`?

These make the basics of the structure of an Arduino program sketch. A structure, holds the program together, and helps the compiler to make sense of the commands entered.

 A compiler is a program that turns code understood by humans into the code that is understood by machines.

There are other loop and control structures as you can see in the following screenshot:

Control Structures

- if
- if...else
- for
- switch case
- while
- do... while
- break
- continue
- return
- goto

These control structures are explained next.

Using loops

Imagine you are teaching your friend to build 6 cm high lego wall. You ask her to place one layer of lego bricks, and then you further ask her to place another layer of lego bricks on top of the bottom layer. You ask her to repeat the process until the wall is 6 cm high.

This process of repeating instructions untill a desired result is achieved is called **Loop**.

 A micro-controller is only as smart as you program it to be.

We move on to the different types of loops:

- **While loop**: Like the name suggests, it repeats a statement (or group of statements) while the given condition is true. The condition is tested before executing the loop body.
- **For loop**: Execute a sequence of statements multiple times and abbreviates the code that manages the loop variable.

- **Do while loop**: Like a while statement, except that it tests the condition at the end of the loop body
- **Nested loop**: You can use one or more loop inside any another while, for or do..while loop.

Now you were able to successfully tell your friend when to stop, but how to control the micro controller? Do not worry, the magic is on its way! You introduce control statements.

- **Break statements**: Breaks the flow of the loop or switch statement and transfers execution to the statement that is immediately following the loop or switch.
- **Continue statements**: This statement causes the loop to skip the remainder of its body and immediately retest its condition before reiterating.
- **Goto statements**: This transfers control to a statement which is labeled . It is no advised to use goto statement in your programs.

 Quiz time: What is an infinite loop? Look up the internet and note it in your inventor-notebook.

The Arduino IDE

The full form of IDE is Integrated Development Environment.

IDE uses a **Compiler** to translate code in a simple language that the computer understands. Compiler is the program that reads all your code and translates your instructions to your microcontroller. In case of the Arduino IDE, it also verifies if your code is making sense to it or not. Arduino IDE is like your friend who helps you finish your homework, reviews it before you give it for submission, if there are any errors; it helps you identify them and resolve them.

Introduction to the Arduino IDE

I am sure by now things look too technical. You have been introduced to SO many new terms to learn and understand. The important thing here is not to forget to have fun while learning. Understanding how the IDE works is very useful when you are trying to modify or write your own code. If you make a mistake, it would tell you which line is giving you trouble. Isn't it cool?

The Arduino IDE also comes with loads of cool examples that you can plug and play. It also has a long list of libraries for you to access. Now let us learn how to get the library on to your computer. **Ask an adult** to help you with this section if you are unable to succeed.

 Make a note of the following answers in your inventor's notebook before downloading the IDE. Get your answers from google or ask an adult. What is an operating system? What is the name of the operating system running on your computer? What is the version of your current operating system? Is your operating system 32 bit or 64 bit? What is the name of the Arduino board that you have?

Now that we did our homework, let us start playing!

How to download the IDE?

Let us now, go further and understand how to download something that's going to be our playground for the following chapters. I am sure you'd be eager to see the place you'll be working in for building new and interesting stuff!

For those of you wanting to learn and do everything my themselves, open any browser and search for Arduino IDE followed by the name of your operating system with **32 bits** or **64 bits** as learnt in the previous section. Click to download the latest version and install!

Else, the step-by-step instructions are here:

1. Open your browser (Firefox, Chrome, Safari):

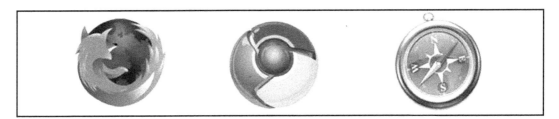

2. Go to `http://www.arduino.cc/` as shown in the following screenshot:

3. Click on the **Download** section of the homepage, which is the third option from your left as shown in the following screenshot:

4. From the options, locate the name of your operating system, click on the right version (32 bits or 64 bits) Then click on **Just Download** after the new page appears:

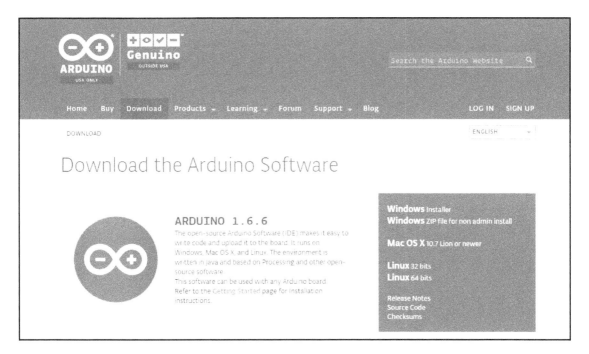

Don't know whether your computer is 64 bits or 32 bits? Use the power of Google to find out! If your system is in fact 32 bits, you will not be able to run a 64-bit IDE on it; if you however have a 64-bit machine, you will still be able to run a 32-bit Arduino IDE on it. I would recommend to double check it and run the right version.

5. After clicking on the desired link and saving the files, you should be able to *double click* on the Arduino icon and install the software. If you have managed to install successfully, you should see the following screens. If not, go back to step 1 and follow the procedure again. The next screenshot shows you how the program will look like when it is loading:

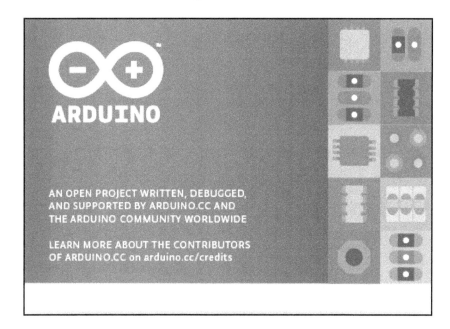

This is how the IDE looks when no code is written into it:

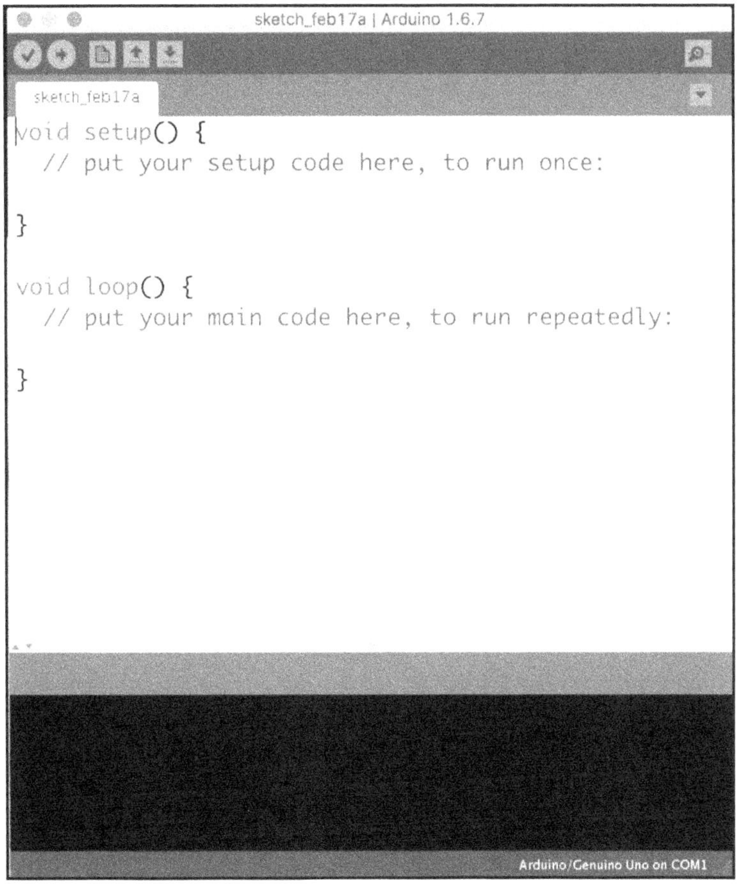

Your first program

Now that you have your IDE ready and open, it is time to start exploring. As promised before, the Arduino IDE comes with many examples, libraries, and helping tools to get curious minds such as you to get started soon. Let us now look at how you can access your first program via the Arduino IDE.

A large number of examples can be accessed in the **File** | **Examples** option as shown in the following screenshot:

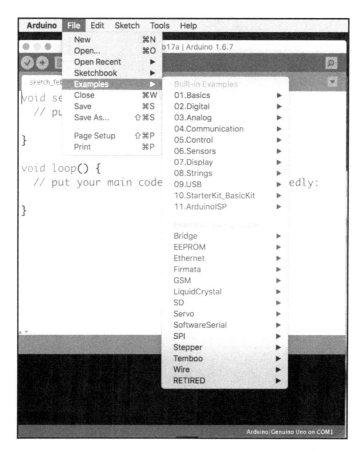

Just like we all have nicknames in school, a program, written in in processing is called a **sketch**. Whenever you write any program for Arduino, it is important that you save your work. Programs written in processing are saved with the extension `.ino`.

The name ino is derived from the last 3 letters of the word Ardu**INO**.

 What are the other extensions are you aware of? (Hint: `.doc`, `.ppt` and so on) Make a note in your inventor's notebook.

Now ask yourself why do so many extensions exist. An extension gives the computer, the address of the software which will open the file, so that when the contents are displayed, it makes sense.

As we learnt above, that the program written in the Arduino IDE is called a **sketch**. Your first sketch is named 'blink'. What does it do? Well, it makes your Arduino blink! You will learn about the hardware in the next chapters, but for now, we can concentrate on the code.

Click on **File** | **Examples** | **Basics** | **Blink**. Refer to next image for this.

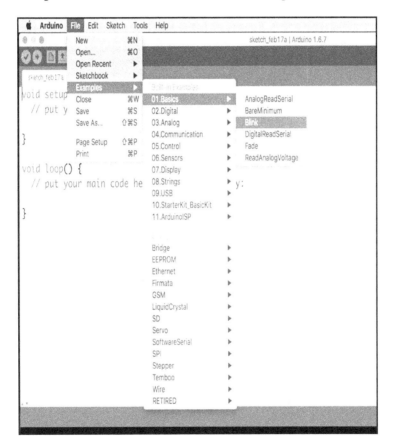

When you load an example sketch, this is how it would look like. In the following image you will be able to identify the structure of code, recall the meaning of functions and integers from the previous section.

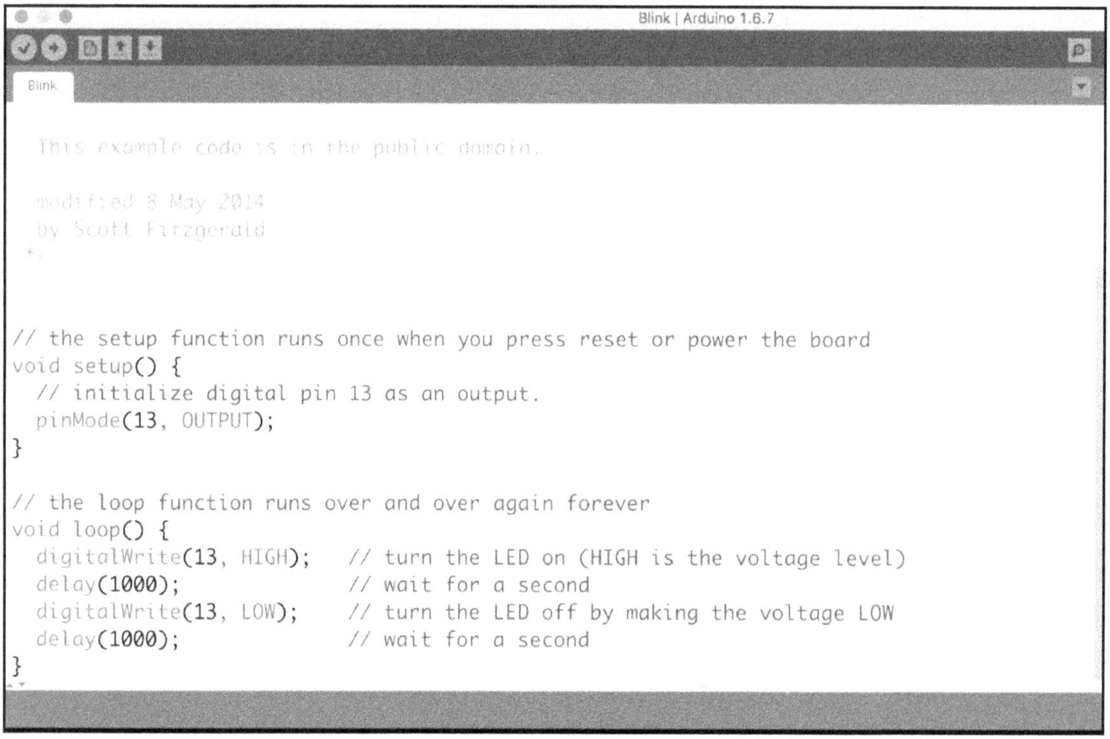

```
Blink | Arduino 1.6.7

Blink

  This example code is in the public domain.

  modified 8 May 2014
  by Scott Fitzgerald
*/


// the setup function runs once when you press reset or power the board
void setup() {
  // initialize digital pin 13 as an output.
  pinMode(13, OUTPUT);
}

// the loop function runs over and over again forever
void loop() {
  digitalWrite(13, HIGH);   // turn the LED on (HIGH is the voltage level)
  delay(1000);              // wait for a second
  digitalWrite(13, LOW);    // turn the LED off by making the voltage LOW
  delay(1000);              // wait for a second
}
```

We learnt that the Arduino IDE is a compiler too! After opening your first example, we can now learn how to document the steps while writing code, so that when we visit back our own code after a long while, we are able to easily understand the steps. The comments are for the human readability only, hence we can hide the information from the microcontroller by using symbols as following:

```
/* your text here*/
```

An alternative to this is as follows:

```
// your text here
```

Comments can also be individually inserted above lines of code, explaining the functions. It is good practice to write comments, as it would be useful when you are visiting back your old code to modify at a later date.

Try editing the contents of the comment section by spelling out your name. The following screenshot will show you how your edited code will look like.

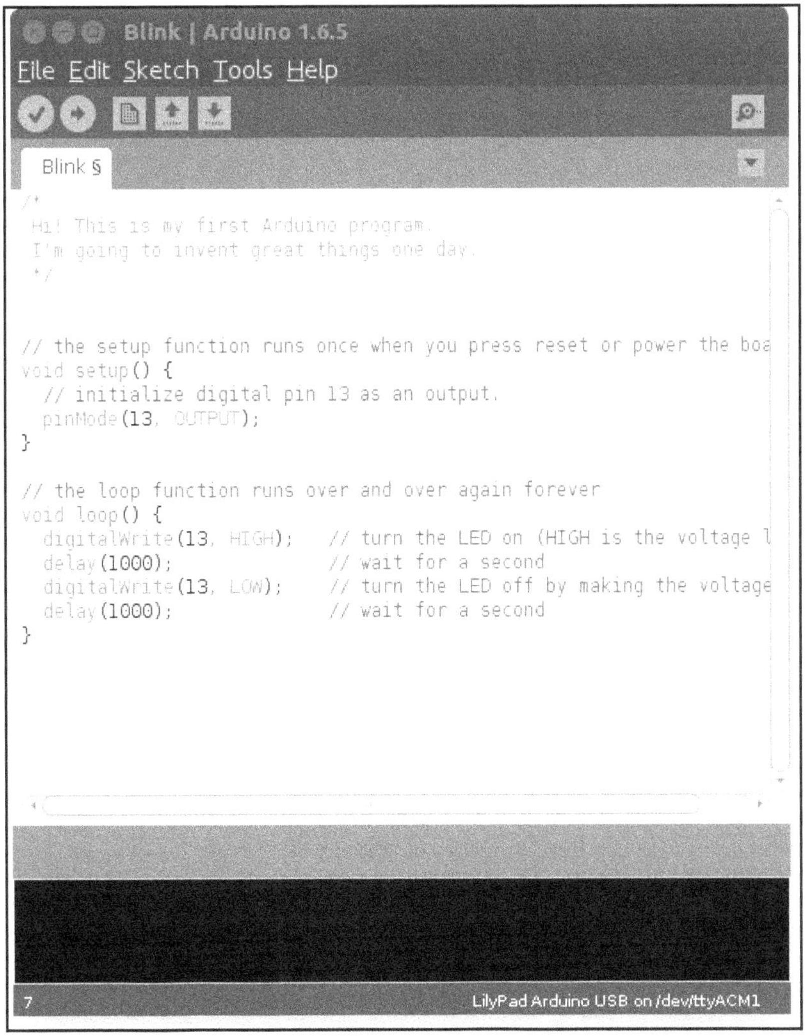

Verifying your first sketch

Now that you have your first complete sketch in the IDE, how do you confirm that your micro-controller has understood exactly what to do?

You do this, by clicking on the easy to locate Verify button with a small ▣.

f you see that the IDE displays the message **Done compiling** (as shown in the following image.) You have successfully written and verified your first code. If not, read the message that the IDE displays and search online to understand more.

Congratulations, you did it!

Saving your first sketch

As we learnt, it is very important to save your work. We now learn the steps to make sure that your work does not get lost.

Now that you have your first code inside your IDE, click on **File** | **SaveAs...**.

The following screenshot will show you how to save the sketch:

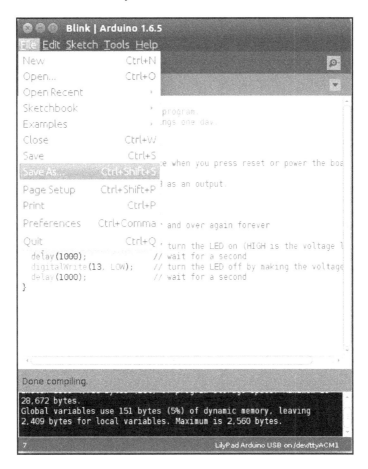

Give an appropriate name to your project file, and save it just like you would save your files from Paintbrush, or any other software that you use.

The file will be saved in a `.ino` format.

Accessing your first sketch

Open the folder where you saved the sketch. Double click on the file you just saved. The program will open in a new window of IDE.

 The following screenshot has been taken from a Mac OS, the file will look different in a Linux or a Windows system.

Summary

Now we know about systems and how logic is used to solve problems. We can write and modify simple code. We also know the basics of Arduino IDE and studied how to verify, save and access your program. Well done, you have made it so far! It's your first step into the world of exploration, discovery and invention! We will learn about components and connections in next chapter that will empower you to start building really cool things!

3
Components and Connections

Things you will learn in this chapter are as follows:

- Electricity
- Current
- Voltage
- Resistors
- Capacitors
- Series and parallel connections
- Sensors
- Physics behind sensors
- Common sensors to be used in the projects
- Making your own sensor

Exploring electricity

When was the last time you spotted lightning? Have you ever felt a jolt while getting out of your car, during winters? How do you think the lights go on immediately after you press the switch?

 Take a balloon, fill it up with air, and close the mouth of the balloon tightly. Now rub the balloon against your dry hair; do this for a few seconds, and take the balloon close to the wall. What happens when you do this? Write it down in your observation notebook.

From static electricity to electric current to the lightning in the sky, these are all examples of various effects of electricity.

Electricity is a physical phenomenon that occurs due to the presence and flow of the electric charge (the unit by which charge is measured is coulomb). Electricity causes many effects that we come across everyday.

All electronic devices–be it our phones, headphones, watches and clocks–all operate on the exact same power source, that is movement of electrons. We know now that the movement of charge (or electrons) causes electricity.

Voltage is the charge difference between two points on a circuit (a circuit is a closed loop where the charge flows from one point to another, usually from a higher charge potential to a lower charge potential).

In similar terms, current is defined as the rate at which the charge follows. Resistance is the tendency of this material to resist the flow of charge. Therefore, whenever we talk about these terms, we are really just talking about the flow of electrons (charge).

We will learn about all of these principals in detail now.

Venturing into voltage

Before we dig into the intricacies of voltage, let's first go through an exercise.

Make a list of five gadgets around you. Under the supervision of an adult, collect the power chord or chargers of these gadgets. Find the sticker on it that shows various numbers. Can you spot it? Use someone's help to do so. Now make a table, and write down the names of the gadgets in one column and numbers that end in a V sign in the other column in your notebook.

What you did above was to write down the voltage rating of the gadgets around you. You will always use this information to identify and understand what the gadgets need to run safely. So, our question arises: what is voltage?

Voltage is the difference in amount of charge between two points in a circuit; this can also be defined as the amount of potential energy between two points on a circuit (or the potential difference between two points). One point has more charge (electrons) than the other. Voltage is scientifically represented by the symbol *V*, and the unit is volt, named after Alessandro Volta, the inventor of first chemical battery.

The best way to understand voltage, current, and resistance is through the water tank example.

Look at the water tank in the following image.

In this example, water represents charge, the pressure of water inside the tank represents voltage, and the flow of water represents current.

The water tank in this case is at a height above the ground. There is an opening or a hose at the bottom of the tank. When you open the hose, the pressure at the hose end can represent voltage. The amount of water in the tank is directly proportional to the pressure at the hose. The more the water, the more the pressure; similarly, the more the charge, the more the voltage.

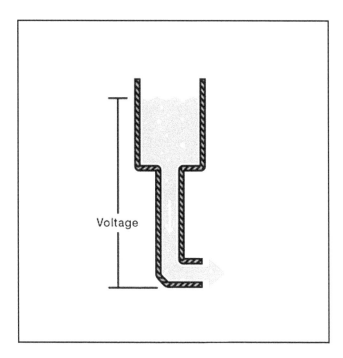

As the amount of water in the tank decreases, the pressure and the rate of flow of water at the tap also decreases.

The same logic applies to batteries that hold charge: the more we use the charge of the batteries, the less the voltage becomes, and hence, the current flowing through it also decreases.

You might have faced this at home, in TV remotes, watches, or gaming consoles that run on batteries. This is significantly visible in flashlights, where the light from the bulb significantly decreases with the drop in voltage. Let's talk about current now.

Conceptualizing current

Before we move on to understanding current, let's go back to the previous exercise and add something more to it.

In the preceding list you made, add another column, and write the numbers that end with an A sign.

What you marked now was the current ratings of the gadgets. Voltage and current ratings written on the devices are also known as power ratings. Simply put, power rating is the highest power inputs (read voltage and current) the appliance is safe to function in.

Let's understand more about current now.

Electrons flow from the negative terminal of the battery (more number of electrons) to the positive terminal terminal of the battery (less number of electrons), just like water flowing from a tank at a higher altitude to a tank at sea level or for a better analogy overhead tank in your house to water tap in your kitchen. Current is caused by the flow of charge (electrons), but conventionally, the direction of current is the opposite direction of the flow of electrons, i.e. positive to negative.

It is important to note that whenever you see a circuit, the flow of current will start from the positive terminal of the battery and end at the negative terminal of the battery.

In the preceding diagram, the amount of water flowing through the tap can be thought of as current. The more the pressure, the more the water flow; this implies that the more the voltage, the more the current.

With water, we would measure the volume of water flowing over a period of time; with charge however, we would calculate the charge flowing through the circuit for a period of time. Since charge is measured is coulombs, current (written as *I*) will be measured as coulombs per second or **Ampere** (**Amp**) after André-Marie Ampère.

Say we have two tanks of the same volume, but the hose in one tank is bigger than the other; water flowing through the one with the bigger hose will be more in quantity than the other. The size of the hose here restricts the amount of water that can flow out.

It should be noted that the water pressure at both the hoses will be the same since the capacity to store charge for both the tanks is the same when the water is not flowing. When the water starts flowing though, the narrower hose will show less flow of water than the wider one as shown in the following diagram:

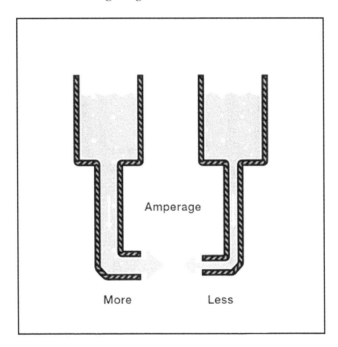

In the current analogy, the current flowing through the narrower hose will be less than the wider one. If we want the current to be the same at both the hoses, we will have to increase the voltage in the tank with the narrower hose as shown in the following diagram:

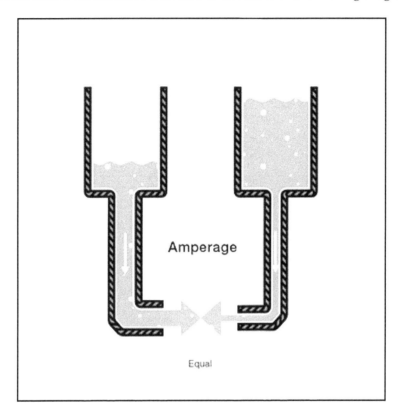

When the pressure (voltage) increases at the end of the narrow hose, it pushes out more water (current). Through this example, we can see that there is a relationship between current and voltage. The voltage in a circuit is directly proportional to the current, but there is also a very important third factor: the size of the hose or resistance. We can now add another term here; the size of the hose is equivalent to the resistance. We will have a look at it in the following sub-section.

Revealing the Resistance

Has it ever happened that your parents asked you to clean your room, but you did not want to? You just wanted to sit and play games instead. That force inside you that doesn't want you to do something is called resistance. Speaking in terms of electronics, resistance is the very basic property of any material that does not want the charge to flow.

Let's consider two water tanks again, one with a wider hose and another with a narrower hose. From the following diagram, we can clearly see that the narrower pipe offers more resistance to the flow of water than the wider hose. We cannot fit as much volume of water in the narrower pipe as we can in the wider pipe, as shown in the following diagram:

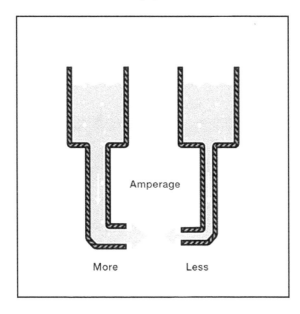

In electrical analogy, we can state that the preceding example is of two circuits with the same voltage (pressure on hose) but different resistances (area of cross section of the hose). The circuit that has a higher resistance shows less amount of charge flow (current) through it. You can understand this better with the following diagram:

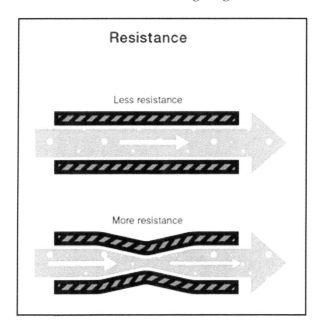

Resistance (represented as R) is measured in Ohm (Ω) after Georg Simon Ohm. Thus, 1 Ohm is the resistance between two points in a circuit when 1 volt of voltage applied across both the points results in 1 ampere of current flowing through the circuit. It is represented by Ω, which is called omega and pronounced Ohm.

The following is the image of what a resistor looks like:

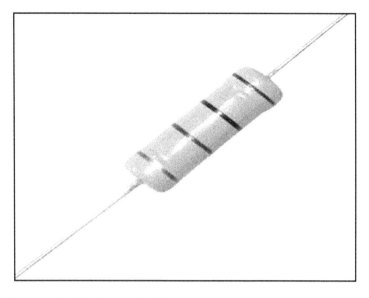

Image source: http://p.globalsources.com/IMAGES/PDT/B1053091783/14W-to-5WS-Carbon-Film-Resistor.jpg

The following table explains the learnings from preceding water diagrams:

Voltage (Pressure)	Current (Flow of water)	Resistance (restriction)
Increases	Increases	Same
Same	Decreases	Increases
Decreases	Same	Decreases

To remember the relationship more easily, just fill in the blanks with the contents from the same row.

Voltage (pressure) _____ and current (flow of water)_____ when resistance (restriction) _____.

Now we move on to another interesting component of electricity, the capacitor.

Comprehending Capacitance

A capacitor is a two-terminal component that has the ability to store electrical energy; they can be compared to a fully charged electric battery. A capacitor only stores charge for a very small time in an electric field. A capacitor's capacity or capacitance (the ability of the component to store charge) is measured in Farad (F), named after Michael Faraday. Capacitance is defined as the ratio of electric charge (Q) on each conductor to the potential difference (V) between both.

You can think of a capacitor as a stretchable membrane (like a balloon or spandex) that is kept between the two ends of a water pipe. Please refer to the following diagram:

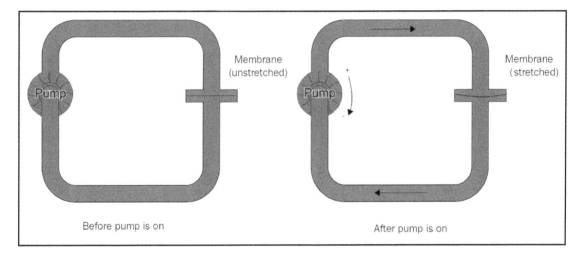

The pump in the system can be compared to a battery.

Initially, the membrane is not stretched, hence the membrane, by itself, has no force in it. As the water starts starts flowing from the pump, it pushes against the membrane and starts stretching it.

While the membrane is stretching, it will push the water on the other side to move a little making it look like water is flowing.

When the membrane reaches its maximum limit, it will exert a pressure equal to the pump's pressure. At this point, the water flow will stop .

This is exactly how capacitors work in electric circuits as well.

The image below shows what a capacitor looks like:

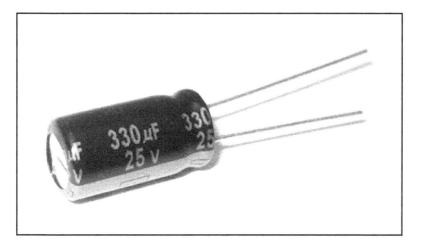

Image source: http://hansenhobbies.com/products/eleccomps/cap_330uf_25v_alu_rad/img1_big.jpg

Understanding Series and Parallel connections

We now already understand the meaning of resistance, capacitance, voltage, and current. Every circuit needs some amount charge to flow in it to function. This need or requirement of current in the circuit is called current requirement. Whenever we apply a voltage to a circuit, the circuit uses/eats or draws current which is equal to voltage applied divided by the total resistance in the circuit. Or 1/R times the voltage applied where R is representative of resistance.

While building your circuit, sometimes you will realize that two different sensors in your circuit have two different types of current requirements; other times you have different voltage requirements. Think of this as the different tactics you use to avoid cleaning the room. In such conditions, we use resistors and capacitors in various combinations to get the desired results.

Series connection

When you have a friend playing with you, isn't it more difficult for you to stop playing and start cleaning, since while you have to clean the house, your friend gets to play? (So unfair!)

A series connection is characterized by all the components connected in a long chain from one terminal of the battery to the other as shown in the diagrams. (Recall from the preceding sections that current flows from the positive terminal of the battery to the negative.)

The following diagram shows resistors R_1 and R_2 that are connected in a series:

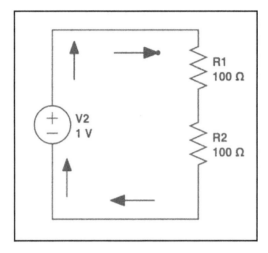

The total resistance in a series circuit is determined by adding all the individual resistances connected in series. Let's get back to the water analogy. The following diagram shows a pump that is pumping water in a water circuit:

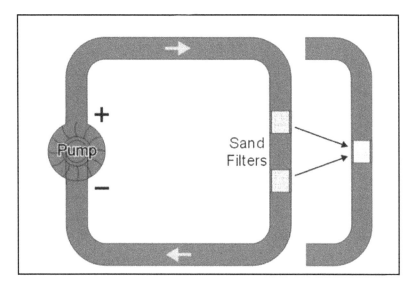

Image source: https://ece.uwaterloo.ca/~dwharder/Analogy/Resistors/

The pipe consists of two sand filters. Since each of the sand filters is going to restrict the flow of water according to the density of the sand on the sand filter, the total resistance going to be offered will be the sum of the individual restrictions. Since restriction here is analogous to resistance in electric circuits, in a circuit with series resistance, the total resistance offered to the circuit is going to be the sum of individual resistances. The current across the resistors remains the same the but voltage gets divided.

Total resistance of the circuit here is $R = R_1 + R_2 + R_3$.

The following diagram shows capacitors C_1 and C_2 connected in series:

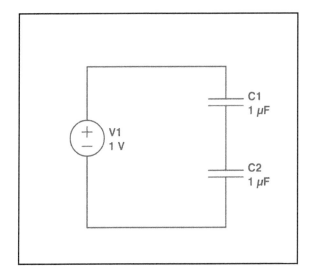

Coming back to the water analogy, consider the following diagram that shows two membranes connected in series:

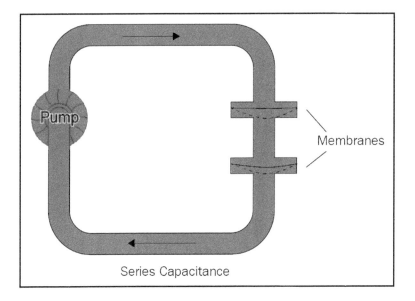

Each membrane, as we already know, restricts the flow of water. When the pressure is applied to membrane 1, it stretches and pushes the water to stretch membrane 2. As membrane 1 reaches its limit, it starts to push back against the water pressure that made it stretch in the first place. At this point, membrane 2 may or may not have reached its maximum stretchable potential.

The total pressure applied in the circuit is equal to the sum of pressures across both the membranes. After a few calculations, it has been found out that the inverse of the total capacitance in the electrical circuits where capacitors are in series is the sum of the inverse of individual capacitance. Mathematically, it is written as: $1/C = 1/C_1 + 1/C_2$.

Parallel connection

Now if your parents ask both you and your friend to stop playing the games and clean the room, since you will not be jealous of your friend anymore, it will be easier for you to go clean the room, right? (Also, this is fair, isn't it?)

A parallel connection is characterized by all the components connected between the same set of electrically common points, as shown in the following diagram. The current in these circuits is divided, but the voltage across the circuit remains the same. Look at the following two diagrams–you will notice that the positive of the battery and one end of both the resistors share a common point; similarly, the negative of the battery and the other end of resistors share a common point.

The following diagram shows resistors connected in parallel. The total resistance of such a circuit will be determined by the following equation:

$1/R = 1/R_1 + 1/R_2$

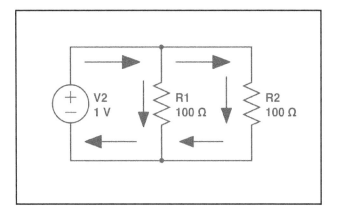

Referring back, if the pipe splits into two and each piece of pipe has the same type of sand filter in it, this is what it is going to look like:

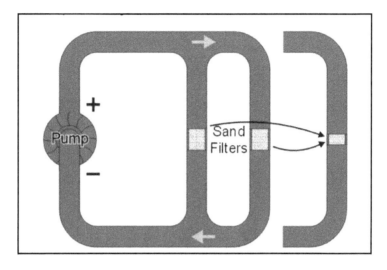

Image source: https://ece.uwaterloo.ca/~dwharder/Analogy/Resistors/

This doubles the surface area through which the water is going to flow. Since there is more surface area, the total resistance being offered to water decreases.

The following diagram demonstrates how the capacitors are connected in parallel. The total capacitance of a parallel-connected capacitor circuit is determined by the total sum of the capacitances:

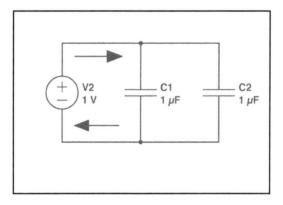

We know both the capacitor membranes are going to stretch and block the flow of water in the individual pipes. Since the total amount of blocking of water is going to increase, we can say that the total capacitance of such a circuit is going to be the sum of individual capacitances. Hence, the equation for calculating the total capacitance will look like this:

$C = C1+C2$

The combination of series and parallel resistors and capacitors is widely used in special circuits called analog circuits. We will learn more about the implementation of these connections in the following chapters. Let's talk about the water circuit analogy of the same parallel circuit:

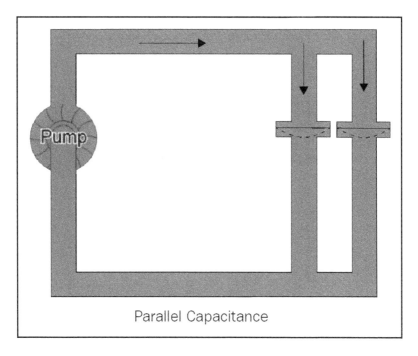

Parallel Capacitance

Let's now go further and learn about something that is in use for everything in today's world. After reading the following section, you will only be surprised!

What are sensors?

Do you remember how we compared the human body to robots in `Chapter 1`, *The World around Us*? Microcontrollers are like the brains in human beings. Similar to human brains, microcontrollers work on a simple input-output concept. So, what is this input-to-output concept?

Anything that is taken in or put in a system is called an input; similarly, output is what is given out of the system.

Look at the following diagram–it shows what a system looks like. This system could be a microcontroller or a human brain:

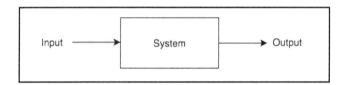

Microcontrollers receive the input information; they process that information and then produce an output. The human brain processes a lot of information too, even before birth. All day, every day, it processes information such as sounds, images, visuals, smells, touch, pain, expressions, and so on. What do you think is the input to the brain? The sense organs in humans provide this input to the brain.

 Find out about some of the various sense organs present in the human body and their functions. Write this down in your notebook.

Sense organs are the inputs to the human brain. Let me tell you how they work. Sense organs have small receptors (a small unit that responds to particular environment condition such as light and smell.) that take the information about various physical conditions to the brain via information channels called neurons. The following block diagram shows how it works in the human brain:

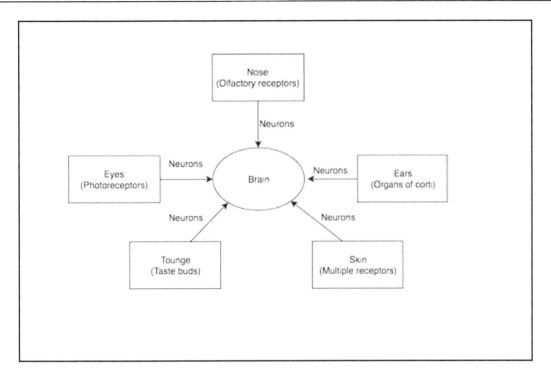

Microcontrollers use various sensors to understand the environment around them. To see, the controllers use cameras; to measure temperature, they use temperature sensors; to measure their orientation and speed, they have special sensors too!

Find out some more examples of sensors. Find out how microcontrollers measure distance, light, and pressure. Write it down in your notebook.

In summary, sensors are devices that help the micro controller learn about the environment around it. Now that we know a little bit about sensors, aren't you curious and excited about how they work? The next section is going to tell you the science behind the sensors.

Physics behind sensors

You know, I always found automatic doors, escalators, and elevators very magical. Every time I would go close to a door and see it open on its own, I would always walk a little away from the door, to the left or to the right, to check at what point I will be close enough for the door to open. It has always been fun.

We interact and use multiple sensors on a daily basis even without knowing their presence. They are present everywhere! Don't you think they make our life simpler?

 Write about at least five different places that you know or think sensors are present. Also, guess the location in the product.

One very important thing that all of us should remember is that all the sensors work on the basic laws of physics. They use physical conditions such as light, temperature, pressure, humidity, and so on, using circuitry within them and converting them into electrical signals.

So, the insides of a sensor will look something like this:

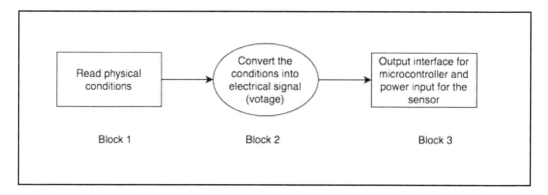

Keep this block diagram in mind; we are going to use this to channel our thoughts when we build our own sensor. Remember the three parts of any sensor: a part that senses physical conditions, a second part that converts that to electrical signals (voltage, in most cases), and a third part that gives the resulting signals to a microcontroller.

 Using the internet, find out what kind of sensors are present in a smart phone in your family, make a list of the sensors in them.

Exploring common sensors

There are so many sensors that we come across every day.

Here is a list of very widely used sensors:

1. Distance sensor (proximity sensor)
2. Temperature sensor
3. Humidity sensor

The very cool thing about sensors in the aforementioned list is that these sensors are used in many things around us, be it smart TVs, laptops, smart watches, home automation systems, or wearable devices. We will learn about these sensors now.

Distance sensor

A distance sensor usually measures the distance between itself and an obstacle using the concept of light waves. A light wave originates from the sensor (from the transmitter of a sensor), bounces back from the obstacle, and is received by the receiver of the sensor. Think of this as you walking in an empty room and shouting something. The voice echoes. That is exactly how the light waves interact and bounce back too, they echo from the object.

In the case of a distance sensor, the first block is just a transmitter-receiver. The second block is what calculates the distance, it measures the time lag between the signal sent and signal received and using laws of physics, identifies the distance. (Going back to the above echo example, if you were to shout in an empty room versus from a mountain top, the time the sound wave will take to reach back to you will be different. Knowing the speed of sound, we can then calculate how far the walls in the room or the next mountain is, the sensor uses the same logic for light waves.) The third block does two things: first, it powers up the sensor, and second, it gives out information about the distance measurements from block two.

You will see proximity sensor widely used in home automation systems, robots, and so on.

Temperature sensor

Block one of a temperature sensor measures the temperature from its surroundings. It consists of resistors that change its resistance based on the temperature. An increase in temperature increases the resistance, and a decrease in temperature decreases the resistance, but not always; there are always exceptions in science, and that's what I love about them the most! You will learn about these exceptions while experimenting.

Using the relationship between voltage, current, and resistance, the second block calculates the voltage and sends this information to block three.

Humidity sensor

Block one of a humidity sensor measures the moisture between the two electrodes of the sensor. Typically, this is used to measure the moisture in soil. The resistance between the two electrodes changes with the moisture–the more the moisture, the less the resistance. We will build this sensor in the last section of the chapter.

Making your own sensor!

Before we start going deeper into this section, you need to know this: you are already an inventor, so you have the power to build all the sensors you want in the world! However, as Spidey's uncle Ben said, with great power comes great responsibility; as an inventor you always follow a process or an approach to solving problems. Remember the notebook you maintain, that's the one!

Write down the following three questions in your notebook:

1. Why?
2. What?
3. How?

Every time you see a problem, ask yourself these questions:

- Why am I doing this?–Find out the answer to this by constantly observing and identifying the problem statements around you. Asking WHY helps you define the problem statement and gives you the reason to stick to the problem statement even when you are in self-doubt. For example, my observation is that the temperature in my city is increasing. Why is it increasing?–It is increasing because of pollution.

- What are you going to do about the problem you found out by asking WHY? In my case, I think by planting a tree and monitoring its health, I could make a very small but significant impact on the environment.
- How are you going to do WHAT you just decided to do? I am going to make a simple moisture indicator to make sure I have optimum amount of water in the pot.

Once you have answered the preceding three important questions, you can start being creative and ideate your HOW. Mind you, answering these questions is not easy; sometimes it takes days or weeks or even months to identify these questions; so don't worry if it's taking you time. Remember, slow and steady wins the race. It is very important to be consistent.

The next important part of this process is feedback. Always ask for feedback from your peers, parents, teachers, and the people who are affected by the problem statement. Everyone has something important to add.

Everyone. in fact. knows about something that you don't, so there is always a huge opportunity to learn from them.

I take constant feedback from my peers and colleagues. While writing the book, I am taking constant feedback from the editor and my co-author to make this book better.

The final and the most important part of this process of inventing is to be iterative. Fake it till you make it! Take small steps, correct them, and move on. With every step, you make your solution better, stronger, and long-lasting.

So now that we know what the process of becoming a successful inventor is, let's dive right into it.

 Adult supervision needed

Aim: To build a soil moisture-level indicator

Requirement: A pot, a plant, two pieces of wire, scissors, scale, two nails, Arduino Uno, breadboard, resistor (10KΩ), jumpers, and so on.

Circuit diagram: The circuit diagram is shown here:

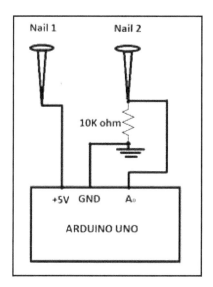

Procedure: The procedure to build a soil moisture-level indicator is as follows:

1. Take a pot and plant a plant in it.
2. Make moisture sensors in the following way:
   - Cut two pieces of wire, each around two inches long, and strip off about half inch on one side of each of the wires. I would recommend you to do this with the help of an adult.
   - Wrap each of the wires around two nails.

The physics behind this sensor is simple. There is an existing resistance between the two nails when they are inserted in the soil. As the moisture in the soil increases, the resistance decreases. Water conducts the charge, the more the water, the more the conductivity and hence resistance to movement of charge decreases.
We should also note that we are not performing any calculation in the sensor, hence there is no block two in this sensor. Now we come to block three.

3. Connect the sensors to Arduino.
   - We make a connection between the ground of the Arduino and the (-) column of the breadboard using a wire.
   - We now connect a wire between the +5V of the Arduino and the (+) column of the breadboard.

- We connect one sensor to the positive column of the breadboard.
- We then connect the other sensor to a new row on the breadboard.
- We connect a 10K Ohm (10 kilo Ohm) resistor to the same row as the moisture sensor and to another new row. This is to restrict the flow of excessive current.
- Connect a wire from Analog input 0 of your Arduino to the same row as the sensor and the resistor; this will enable us to read input values from pin number A0.
- Connect the other end of the resistor (in the new row) to the ground. Please refer to the following diagram for a better understanding of the circuit.

Connection diagram:

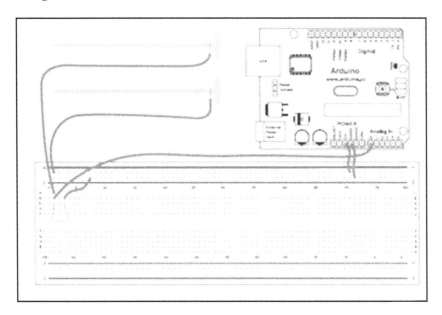

Now, before we start writing the code, since we are inventors here, here is another rule we should always remember: never reinvent the wheel. If you can find a piece of technology or a code about something you are trying to work on, just build on top of that. Here, I am going to introduce one of the best ways to use the example code. You already know how to navigate to them, right? If you need a refresher, go back to Chapter 2, *Systems and Logic*.

Here is what we know:

- The sensor we have built will give us some kind of variable resistor values.

This means we have to read the values from the Analog pins.

- Examples from your Arduino software have the sample code of Analog Input.

This means if we open this example, we will be able to directly upload the code to the Arduino and just start reading the values being sent by the sensor.

Always remember that when you start with a project and you don't know how to exactly go about it, break the problem statement down into pieces and start solving for each of the pieces. Hereon, look at an example that you think is the closest to what you are trying to solve.

Next you will see the code that is inspired from the Analog Input example. I made a few changes to make it look much simpler:

```
Moisture

int sensorPin = A0;
int mSensor = 0;

void setup() {
  // put your setup code here, to run once:
  Serial.begin(9600);
}
void loop() {
  // put your main code here, to run repeatedly:
  mSensor = analogRead(sensorPin);
  Serial.print("Value of the sensor is: ");
  Serial. print(mSensor);
  delay(500);
}
```

Code:

```
int sensorPin = A0;
int mSensor = 0;

void setup() {
 // put your setup code here, to run once:
 Serial.begin(9600);
}
void loop() {
 // put your main code here, to run repeatedly:
 mSensor = analogRead(sensorPin);
 Serial.print("Value of the sensor is: ");
 Serial.print(mSensor);
 delay(500);
}
```

The preceding code is going to continuously read values from the sensor and print it on the serial monitor every half second. Serial monitor is part of the Arduino Software is used for all communications between Arduino boards and computer and other devices.

We will learn about how to start writing our own programs in the coming chapters.

Summary

In this chapter, you learned about the building block of circuits. You now know about voltage, current, resistance, and the relationship between them. You learned about various combinations of resistors and capacitors and how they collectively work in circuits. You also learned about the physics behind sensors, you now know what process to follow to solve any problem in the world, and most importantly, you built your own sensor!

In the next chapter, you are going to learn everything about Arduino, how to write code, how to tinker with examples and attach sensors to Arduino. I am super excited. Are you?

4
The Magic Wand

Things you will learn about in this chapter are as follows:

- Microcontroller
- The process of coding a microcontroller
- Power supply
- Integrated Development Environment for Arduino
- Inside the working of a microcontroller
- Open-source software and hardware

Demystifying microcontroller

We will start exploring the microcontroller by comparing it to something we already know about: our brain. Let's refer to the following diagram. You have already seen this diagram in the last chapter, but this one has more clues to demystify the microcontroller:

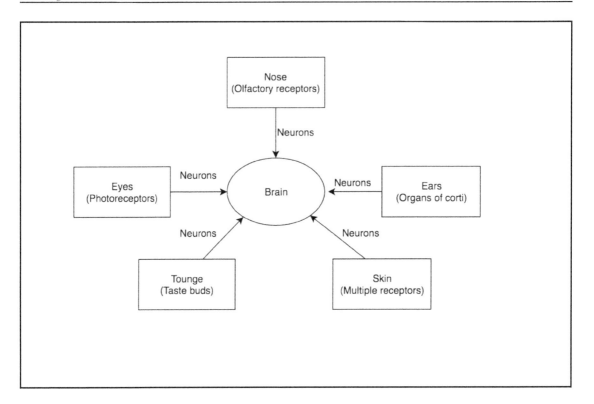

Close your eyes for a moment, and think about everything you know about yourself: your hobbies, things you like, things you do, and so on. Write it down in your observation notebook. We are going to learn about ourselves today!

Microcontrollers are a fascinating piece of technology created by our species. They consist of three major parts; they are:

- **Processor core:** This processes everything; it is is the brain of the microcontroller
- **Program memory:** This consists of instruction and acts as memory for the controller, just as our brain has memory.
- **Inputs and Outputs**: This is used to process external data. This is also where external devices connect all of which are controlled by the micro controller.

We will learn about these in detail. But before that, there is something you should know. A microcontroller is basically a miniaturization of our own brains! Let that sink in for a moment. Got goosebumps yet? Do you want to how our microcontrollers are inspired from the brain? Let's talk about it.

The brain of a microcontroller is its processor core. The bigger the processor core, the more efficiently it will function and execute the instructions given to it. A brain itself has various parts. Here is what we know about our brains.

Memory

Every morning when you get up and go to brush, take a bath, and get ready, have you ever wondered how you do most of these activities without really thinking about them? Do you learn to do these activities every day, or do you somehow just know how to do them? When you meet new people, you ask for their names, and soon after, you remember their names, don't you? You somehow know how to walk, how to talk, how to shake hands, how to read, right? Ever thought about how you just remember these things?

A part of our brain is responsible for storing information; we call it memory. Very similar to our brains, microcontrollers also have a tiny space where the code we write is stored.

Timers

Here is another question to you: ever thought about how you just wake up in the morning and fall asleep at night? Doesn't it feel like our bodies have a clock of its own? Somehow it knows what to do when. While we look at clocks and watches, our bodies have their own system.

This ability of our body to do things at certain points in time is sometimes loosely termed as our biological clock, too, and a part of our brain is dedicated to keeping track of everything we do, time-wise. Microcontrollers also need a system through which they can keep a check on everything they are working on. We call these clocks timers. You know, one of the many things I love about microcontrollers is that they are never late! One thing for you to remember here is that a micro controller is going to be late only if you make it.

Arithmetic and logic unit

You might have friends or family who are really good at Math and doing quick calculations. Did you know that the left part of our brain is responsible for that? We call this part the logical part of the brain. The right part of our brain controls all the creative things we do; painting, music, and a lot more creative activities are controlled by this part of our brain.

Microcontrollers, as we know by now, need to do a lot of calculations too. The section inside the microcontrollers that controls these activities is called the Arithmetic and Logic Unit or ALU.

Analog to Digital converters

The microcontrollers understand only binary that is 1s and 0s which is called the Digital format. So anything that we want out micro controller to understand needs to be broken down to 1s an 0s. It could be the color of the sky or temperature of water or just a simple multiplication. (I encourage you to learn how to convert out analog world to binary using the power of the internet. For example what is the binary(or digital format) of the number 20?) Our world however is Analog(we will learn more about it in the next few lines). When we work with sensors that read the physical world, we have to convert that into a format that our microcontroller understands.

For this, our microcontrollers are equipped with Analog to Digital Converters. We have Analog pins labeled A0 to A5 that can read the analog input voltage and convert that into a digital signal. Refer back to `Chapter 3`, *Components and connections,voltage section*. A micro-controller denotes 1 as a high voltage (usually 5V in Arduino) and 0 as low voltage (usually 0V in Arduino). The highest value ADC that can count at 5V is 1023; at 0V it is close to 0. So, if an input signal is of 2.9 volts, we use the ADC to find the value closest to either 0 volts or 5 volts for the system to understand.

Stretch both of your arms wide open. Now, using both your arms and your upper body, if you had to show what a wave looks like, how would you show it? Try it for a couple of times.

The following diagram shows how I would do it:

In nature, when we work with signals in their natural form, this is exactly how they exist too, in a wavy form. It's not exactly the wave I made, but you get the idea, right?

The length and the style of these waves are very different from each other. When we want to read these values using a microcontroller, we will have to covert these waves in the format our micro controllers understand, which consists of 1s and 0s.

The following diagram shows how we can consider values low and high on ADC values:

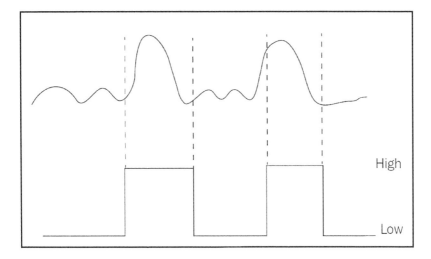

You will notice that anything in the preceding wave that is higher than the rest is considered high, and everything else is considered low.

The following image shows the Analog Pins on an Arduino Uno:

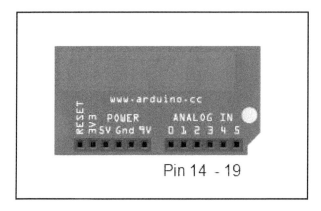

Input and output lines

Neurons in our brain carry input signals form the sense organs and output signals to respective part of the body. When I see my friends, I wave my hands to greet them. Neurons take signals from my eyes to the brain, and then the brain sends signals to my hands to wave. Similarly, microcontrollers have input and output lines to connect to sensors to read the inputs and various output lines to connect to the motors or anything else that we want to actuate.

You could also consider input lines as the entry gates to a mall and output lines as exit gates. More often than not, entry gates and exit gates are different from each other.

Registers

Registers are very similar in nature to memory. Registers in microcontrollers have very specific hardware-related functions in addition to memory. Hardware registers are used to act like an interface between software and peripherals. They can be imagined as tiny slots that can be used to give data to or take data from. Some registers are used for storing data temporarily, and they might not be physically connected to the pins, but other are physically connected to input/output pins, serial ports, and so on. Talking to these registers is how we perform operations such as running a motor or reading a value from a sensor.

There are three kinds of registers connected to every pin in Arduino: one register is for providing data direction, which means either input or output. You will see this being used at the `pinMode()` declaration in the code.

The second register is called the PORT register. When a pin has been set up as output, the `PORT` register is used. This is used when we use the `digitalWrite()` function.

The third register is called the PIN register. When a pin has been set up to read values, it uses the `PIN` register to read values. This is used during the `digitalRead()` function.

To break this down, all we need to remember is that Arduino has three different slots that interface the hardware (all input / output pins, memory, ALU, and so on) to the software being written in the micro controller.

Coding the microcontroller – the process

Introduction

I am assuming that we already have the Arduino Software installed and setup in our computers. If you haven't yet, refer back to `Chapter 2`, *Systems and Logic*, and you will be able to find out how to do that.

 We can always refer to `https://www.arduino.cc/en/Guide/HomePage` for more help.

Now comes the part where you will understand why this chapter is called *The Magic Wand*. Remember how I told you about a process you must follow for any problem statement you might have faced? Don't remember? That's okay, head back to the last chapter and have a quick look at it again.

Let's understand more about the skeleton (or the structure) of code we should follow when we write Arduino code.

Remember how I keep talking about having a process? The process or method that you follow while writing code for Arduino is by identifying two things:

- The part of the code you want to run just once
- The part of the code you want to keep running

Let's take an example. When you see someone using a washing machine, they open the door to the machine only two times: once when they put the clothes inside and later when they take it out. Let's consider the case in which you have to wash clothes. What do you do?

You open the door of the machine, put the clothes inside, and close the door. Do you keep doing this again and again? No. You do it just once for one set of clothes. So this case is a good example of point 1.

What do you do next? You give the machine instructions, and the machine starts rotating the clothes inside with water and detergent that you have added to it. The machine keeps doing this forever (or in this case, for a set period of time). This is a good example of case number 2.

To recap it quickly, any action that you want the system to perform once and only once will be considered 1, and any action that you want the system to keep performing will be considered 2.

How does this translate in code though? Let's see what 1 could mean to us when writing code. If we want to assign the pins for inputs and outputs, set a timer or declare the names for the pins, we will declare it just once. The loop in which you declare this is called **void setup()**. The following screenshot shows you what the loop looks like:

```
void setup() {
  // put your setup code here, to run once:

}
```

When you want to do calculations from continuously flowing inputs or continuously flowing outputs, such as LEDs or motors, you have to keep running the code without stopping. Any code that needs to keep running continuously has to be written in `void loop()`. The following screenshot shows what a void loop looks like:

```
void loop() {
    // put your main code here, to run repeatedly:

}
```

In other words, Microcontroller will follow everything written under `void setup()` just once, and whatever is written under `void loop()` forever. So if there is no `loop()`, controller will executer your instruction only once and sit back and relax and since the microcontroller runs so fast, you won't be able to even see it. Now that we know how loops work, let's talk about how to approach writing code.

We will start by naming. Do you know why we name things? It is easier for our brain to remember the object that we have named. How does the brain do this? The brain takes the tag or the name we give any object and stores that tag in a register inside the brain.

Information of any sort is called data. We should remember this very carefully.

So now every time we will use the tag or the name, the brain will look for the memory associated with that tag.

We know now that microcontrollers are nothing but a miniaturization of our brain. So a microcontroller also saves the tags or names of various pins/sensors/numbers/words in it in a very similar way.

Data could be of many types: in the form of a picture, numbers, characters, emojis, and so on. So in the computer world, to make things easy for us, we have all agreed that data is going to be of three different types only.

If the data is Yes or No (1 or 0 for the computer to understand), it will be called Boolean Data. We denote that in code as *bool*.

If the data is a character (a,b,c,d, and so on) or a string (names such as Arduino, 12arduino432, 123123124, and so on), it will be called Textual Data. This data, as you can see, has some kind of a text involved or a long sequence of numbers within quotes. We denote this in code as *char*.

If the data is some sort of a number (1, 2, 1.23, 3.45, -12, and so on), it will be called Numerical Data. Numerical data again is of multiple types. But to make it easy for us, we are only going to remember one type of data, which is *int*. We will start using more data types as we start writing more code in the next chapters.

Now that we know how many types of data there are, let's take one last step to get ready to write code. We need to understand the concept of variable and constant. What keeps changing is called a variable, such as age, or the amount of chocolate I can eat all at once. Simple enough?

What doesn't change is called a constant, such as the number of apples in a dozen, or the number of centimeters in a meter, or my liking for chocolate.

When we are talking in terms of code, we will edit that definition a little bit. Any datum (singular for data) that changes during the course of running the code is called a variable. Any datum that does not change during the course of running the code is called a constant.

So if we want to name our pins and we don't want the names or the pin numbers to change, we can declare them as follows:

```
intnameYouLike = A0;
```

In the preceding code, *int* is the variable type, it's a number. I know it could be confusing since A0 is not a number, but technically it is, since A0 is connected to a pin number on the Arduino board. Mind = Blown, right?

Or take a simpler example:

```
intsensorPin = 9;
```

If we want to declare a name that could hold value that keeps changing, we will declare it as follows:

```
int j;
```

Declaring all the variables and names that you will be using in your code at the beginning of the code is a good practice. Also there can be no spaces in the variable names. You could choose *iLikeVanillaIceCream* as a name but not *I like Vanilla Ice Cream*. You must remember that writing code is an art. Much like playing the piano or learning pottery, it takes some time to learn the good practices and a lot of practice to become good at it.

What's so good about coding? EVERYBODY can learn how to code!

 Using the internet, find out how to write constant and variable declarations in your code.

Do you remember how to run basic examples in your code? I am sure you do. But just in case you don't, go back to chapter 1 or 2 (find out which one) and find out how we run examples!

Remember we just learned about registers? All we need to do to access another register in LED blink example is to declare another pin, say pin 3, declare it, and add it in the following code:

```
// the setup function runs once when you press reset or power the board
void setup() {
  // initialize digital pin 13 and pin 3 as an output.
  pinMode(13, OUTPUT);
  pinMode(3,OUTPUT);
}

// the loop function runs over and over again forever
void loop() {
  digitalWrite(13, HIGH);// turn the LED on (HIGH is the voltage level)
  digitalWrite(3,HIGH);
  delay(1000);              // wait for a second
  digitalWrite(13, LOW);    // turn the LED off by making the voltage LOW
  digitalWrite(3,LOW);
  delay(1000);              // wait for a second
}
```

Code:

```
// the setup function runs once when you press reset or power the board
void setup() {
  // initialize digital pin 13 and pin 3 as an output.
  pinMode(13, OUTPUT);
  pinMode(3,OUTPUT);
}
// the loop function runs over and over again forever
void loop() {
  digitalWrite(13, HIGH); // turn the LED on (HIGH is the voltage level)
  digitalWrite(3,HIGH);
  delay(1000); // wait for a second
  digitalWrite(13, LOW); // turn the LED off by making the voltage LOW
  digitalWrite(3,LOW);
  delay(1000); // wait for a second
}
```

Process

The following are the steps of process:

1. Identifying the what: We always start by identifying what we are trying to do here. Go back to the previous chapter to go through the process again.

   Now that we have identified the WHAT. We find out how we are going to do it. Let's take an example. I need to create a burglar alarm. So I have identified I need to build it, reason for that being someone eats chocolates from my desk when I am away. I keep the chocolates in my drawer. How do I go about building this?

2. Breaking down the how: I need a mechanism to trigger an alert when the drawer is opened.

   Let's break the aforementioned sentence even further. What are the key words here? **trigger an alert** and **drawer is opened**. From this, we know we have two action points.

3. Identifying how to solve for action points. Identify the closest connection to what you know: We will now attempt to solve for the individual phrases. Let's see the first one.

- **Trigger an alert** : We know this action depends on opening the drawer. We know we should create an alert that informs me of my drawer being opened when I am not around. This means the alert could be a loud sound or a lot of LEDs glowing together around my desk so someone sitting next to me could identify that there is something wrong.

  I like the idea of triggering the LEDs better. Let's pick that. So, we are going to light the LEDs when the drawer is open.

  What does this translate to in coding concept? It translates to: we will be writing code to light LEDs, which happens on a condition.

  Let's break it down to an example we know of. Do you know of an example where we light up the LEDs or blink the LEDs? Yes, you do!

  Now let's solve for the second one:

- **Drawer is opened**: How could we find out that the drawer's opened? Let's think about this. What if we could create a circuit which when interrupted, sends a signal (Boolean 1 or 0) to the Arduino code? Would that help? Yes it would.

  What kind of circuit could that be?

  Let's think about this a little more. Have we worked on a similar concept before–a concept in which a circuit was being formed or broken? Do you remember building the soil sensors? Do you get a hint now?

  I urge you to take a 10-minute break now. Close you eyes, take a deep breath, and try to remember what we did when were building soil sensors. Come back here when you can remember that.

  We built the soil sensors on the basic science of the circuit being complete. We can use the same concept here too. Instead of pouring water to complete the circuit, we will use another technology. But let's look at how it will reflect on the code. The logic of this action is going to be the same as that of the soil sensor. Isn't that just magical? Just think about this, two different problem statements, two different applications, but both have a very similar logic structure!

4. Testing individual logics and understanding power supply needs: The best way of tackling a big problem is attacking small parts of it and solving for them.

    So whenever we are going to solve for a problem statement, after the third step, we are going to test individual logics first with the circuits, make sure they have no syntax errors, they are logically correct, and only then move to step 5.

    We have to be cognizant of the fact that power supply is the most important part of the circuit. We need to be sure about how much current we require for all the peripherals and if our Arduino board is capable of providing that.

*   **Consolidating all the logics**: This could be either the most challenging or the easiest thing to do, depending on how well we perform step 4. This step is like putting the right pieces of a puzzle together. We will not talk about it here. We will start applying this step in the next chapters.

*   **Testing and packaging the project**: This is last and the most important step. We will test the total setup. We will document the code so when we look at the code a few months from now, we still remember how it works and what the logic flow while building it was.

    We will make sure all the connections are done properly, no loose connections are left. All the GND and 5V connections are clean, and there is no possibility of a short circuit.

Power supply

We all know what power is, right? Okay, let's not assume; let's quickly go back to Chapter 2, *Systems and Logic* and refresh our knowledge about power. Come back here once you have read that.

All set? Great!

Now that we know what power is, let's find out why it is important to us. Arduino boards have an LED that switches on every time we connect with our computer, have you noticed that? No? Try it once, it will have a quick blink of some sort.

Every time you connect you Arduino board to the computer, you are powering it up. The USB port in the computer gives out 5 volts and some amount of current.

 Find out how much current comes out of the USB port and write it down in your observation notebook.

An Arduino board typically functions on a 5V and 200mA power input. If the board is not given that much input, it won't power up at all, which means you won't be able to use it.

What happens if there is more current or voltage given to the board?

To make sure that the microcontroller gets the same amount of power in all the conditions, there is a voltage regulator on the board and a lot of resistors to make sure current is regulated. What does regulation mean though?

It simply means that if the amount of input is less than the required input, a device is going to collect the input till it reaches the required input level and then supply.

If, on the other hand, the input is more than required, a device is going to reduce the input till it matches the required input level. In this process, since there is going to be a lot of work done by the device, it is going to lose energy in the form on heat. So when we have to convert 12V to 5V, we will see our Arduino board heating up. This is normal. If we give the board 20V input, it will heat up excessively. While the internal regulator in Arduino is capable of doing a conversion of up to 20V to 5V, it is not recommended to do so.

When high voltage is applied, a lot of electrons can rush inside. To stop them from rushing in, the regulator has to apply a lot of force against them. In this process, a lot of electrons get angry, and since they are mad, they have a lot of energy in them. This energy is released in the form of heat.

We know how the regulator works inside the microcontroller. But that's not it, remember the concept of AC and DC current? Go back to chapter 2 for a quick review on it.

So what do you think? Inside the microcontroller, do we work with DC voltages or AC voltages?

Another question to you: how would you power up an Arduino with the power supply at your house? It works on a 110V (or 220V) AC depending on which part of the world you live in. How do you regulate that to 5V?

The answer is simple, and we all already know about it. We use a adapter for powering up the board. These adapters are same as the mobile chargers that convert 110V AC to a voltage range that the Arduino board can operate in.

 Find out how you read the power ratings of an adapter. You have done a similar exercise before. Write down the power rating on your mobile phone charger under an adult's supervision. Find out if your laptop charger could be used to power an Arduino. If yes, how, and if not, why not.

Power capabilities of an Arduino board are pretty impressive too! We can create self sufficient circuits using just an Arduino board. The voltage output from pins is about 5Vs and total current we can pull as an output from an Arduino is only 200mA. This means that if 1 LED requires say 20mA, we can only light up a maximum of 10 LEDs, not more.

Let's use the IDE

Before we start, what is an IDE? **IDE** stands for **Integrated Development Environment** (it is nothing but a fancy name for software!). It contains a lot of useful tools we will use hereon for all our projects.

We write code in the IDE, and we call it a sketch. IDE converts the code we write to a language that our Arduino boards understand; this process is called compilation. Before doing that, it checks for any errors we might have made in the code.

IDE can only check for syntax errors not the logical errors. Syntax errors are the errors in the arrangement of words while we type that code. This arrangement should match the norms that are defined by the language. IDE is not going to let you proceed to upload the code until all the syntax errors are corrected by you. Most of the mistakes I have done have been in missing out on writing ; at the end of each line of code.

Other syntax errors include not declaring the variables properly, using variable names in the code without declaring them in advance, and so on.

Now let's get into more details about the IDE.

When you open the Arduino IDE, this is what the top section of the IDE will look like:

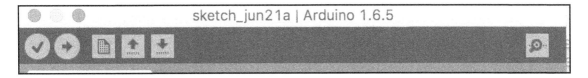

The red, yellow, and green buttons are to close, minimize, and maximize the IDE window respectively. I use a Mac, so the position of the buttons might change if you are using a Windows or Linux Machine.

The following section consists of a lot of very useful buttons:

Buttons	Description
	This is the verify button. Its job is to check for any errors.
	Is the upload button. It compiles the code that we have written and uploads it to the configured board. We will learn in the following section that Arduino IDE lets us work with a variety of boards, both from Arduino (called Genuino outside USA) and anyone else who has built a board compatible with the Arduino. Isn't that phenomenal?
	Is the new button. It creates a new sketch for you whenever you want.
	Is the open button. It shows a menu of all the sketches in your sketchbook. Sketchbook, as you may have already guessed, is the place where all your sketches are saved.
	Is the save button. It saves your code.
	Is the Serial Monitor button. It opens the serial monitor. We will learn more about the Serial Monitor soon.

You can find more tools within the five menus: File, Edit, Sketch, Tools, Help.

Here I would like you to experiment again. As part of building a process, we will learn how to use online resources to find solutions to problem we come across.

 Here is a link `https://www.arduino.cc/en/Guide/Environment` that explains, in detail, what each of the aforementioned tools do. Find out more about these tools and start writing down your learning in your notebook.

Inside the working of a microcontroller

What happens inside a microcontroller almost looks like magic. Think about it for a second: an Arduino Uno is executing 125,000 instructions per second. It is that fast! You may ask what an instruction is. Every line written in code is basically an instruction for the core processor of the microcontroller. So when we say `digitalRead()`, that is an instruction.

Let's take an analogy to understand how a microcontroller works.

There are worms on the earth. Each worm is equivalent to an instruction or an operation that needs to be done.

There is a bird in the sky. Bird is going to take these worms to the chicks in the nest.

Chicks (or the core) eat the worms (or execute an operation/instruction). The mother bird has to keep bringing the worms to the chicks. The system is going to be fast when the chicks have already finished eating the worm before the mother bird brings in more worms.

This means that an operation needs to be executed before another operation comes to the core. The bigger the core, the faster it can finish the operation. If the operation is too big, the core will have to break the operation into many pieces. If the core can only break down the operation to eight pieces (small core) instead of 16 pieces (bigger core), it will be very slow. The larger the core, the more data it can process at the same time.

The following steps will explain the full cycle:

1. Operation is fetched from program memory.

    This operation will fetch data from input/output pins, or storage, depending on what operation it is. This means one line of the program is being executed. This data will be in the form of 1s and 0s.

2. Operation is executed by core while new operation is being fetched.

    This cycle will keep going until all the operations are executed by the core.

    On resetting the microcontroller, the same cycle starts again. The following diagram represents the cycle:

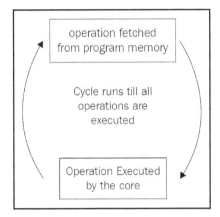

Congratulations! Now you know how the microcontroller works! In the following chapters, we will be using this knowledge to understand the execution of our code.

Let's now talk about a very important concept or philosophy called open source.

Open-source hardware and software

What's your favorite dish? Do you like pudding? My mum makes this delicious pudding that has chocolate chips in it. Every time I taste it, it has the right amount of sugar in it and the perfect amount of a very gingery flavor that makes a tickle on my tongue, always.

My mum tells me that this recipe was given to her by her grandma, and the original recipe didn't have chocolate chips in it and there was no cardamom either. Over the ages, as she acquired new tastes, she kept adding or subtracting things depending on her mood sometimes, sometimes mine. Isn't that a beautiful thing? Wouldn't it be amazing if you could cook a dish exactly like your mum did?

When you can look into how something was built and the source (or the recipe) is made available and can be modified and redistributed, it is called open source. If it is in the hardware domain, it is called open-source hardware, if it is in the software domain, it is called open-source software.

Without Arduino being open source, I would have never been able to learn or build. Open source has led to the formation of support communities for everything we do. If you google *how to build a burglar alarm with Arduino*, you will find a lot of links. On Arduino.cc, instructables, magazine links, blogs, it is this community that keeps the world on innovation fueled up. Did you know there are kids your age who are building satellites that would have taken them years to build without experts pouring their knowledge out in the open. Their designs, their code, their process is available for anyone to learn from and build upon. Open source software and hardware has saved lives by helping build medical devices that help in diagnosing diseases.

Personally, I share everything I work on with the community, to learn from the experts in the domain, to identify what could have I done better, to truly make a difference. I urge you to share what you do with people around you too.

While open source fuels innovation, patents (and other methods) help you keep it a secret. There is always a debate between the open-source communities and the communities that patent their work about who is right.

I would like you to know that there is no right or wrong here. Sometimes, people patent their work so that they could get a return (in terms of money or recognition) for the hard work they have put in coming up with a piece of technology or a method. That is totally fine. No one should be judged. You can get both of the aforementioned by open sourcing your projects too. Did you know Elon Musk (co-founder of Tesla, SpaceX, and Solar City), open sourced all his patents for the world to learn how to make the most efficient and fastest electric vehicles?

At the end of the day, remember this: if you want people to learn from your methods and mistakes, you can choose to share your work with them; if you want people to use what you have built but not know how you have built it, you can choose to keep it a secret.

Open source is to enable people like you and me make changes to the things we want, giving due credit to the original creator and sharing it further.

Summary

We learned a lot of important things in this chapter. Starting from how a microcontroller is made very similar to a human brain to what should be the approach towards coding a microcontroller. We then learned the importance of the power supply in Arduino, how it is very important to know the operating voltages on Arduino. We then learned how to use the Arduino software–some important parts of the software–and how to look up for help online. We learned about how a microcontroller works internally, and finally, we learned about what is open-source hardware and software. In the next chapter, we will learn how to finally take all the learnings into code and start working on our first project. I am super excited about this, are you too?

5
Hello World!

Things you will learn about in this chapter are as follows:

- Arduino startup
- Switches – Push Button
- Sensors – LDR
- Coding the concept to life

Hey Arduino! Let's get to work

It has been quiet a journey hasn't it? We started out 5 chapters ago, to learn how this magical thing called Arduino works, and here we are today, 4 chapters old. Let's take a moment and give ourselves a round of applause. Here are a few things I know we know. One, we know what a problem means, and how do we identify it. Two, we know how we approach a problem statement. Three, we know the basics of electronics and micro controllers well. Four, we know what sensors are and we also know how to build our own! Five, we also know how to use Arduino IDE and open up examples in it.

Now this is the time when we weave all of these learnings together and start building!

We are going to do an additive process of learning. We will learn how can we make a very *light sensitive* bot. We will use a lot of steps to reach our final goal.

Let's break down the final goal a little bit more. We are going to make a Light Sensitive bot. Let's break down the word Light Sensitive further. How do you do just this? We must use a sensor that reacts to light right? So we are going to chose a sensor that understands and measures light.

Say this bot is understanding when there is light, how would the bot show it is light sensitive to us? If your friend was to pinch you, what would you do? Scream a little bit to let everyone know about it right? Its our natural reaction. We will use the same concept for a bot.

Now let's think about what have we learnt so far that can be directly applied here. Hmm, we know how to build a soil sensor, can we use that here? No.

We know how to blink an LED using the LED blink example. Hey LED could be a way for the bot to let the humans know right? Perfect. Let's use this then.

So this is what we have decided. The bot will be sensitive to light, we will use a sensor that understands and measures light for this. Once light falls on the bot, we will use an LED to inform that humans that bot is sensitive to the light that has fallen on it. Perfect.

Let's draw this out shall we so that we don't forget, at any point, what the aim of this is?

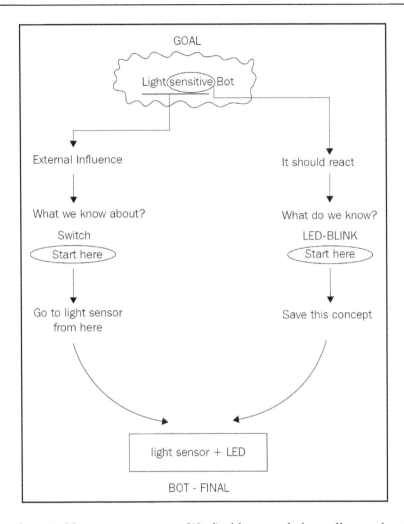

This drawing above is like a treasure map. We find keys and clues all over the map. But no one keeps the clues for us. We will have to build individual concepts to take out the key learnings that we will implement next. Most important part of this map is that we break down every piece of the problem in the things we already know and start from there.

In life, it could be an electronics problem or otherwise. You always draw yourself a map and see what can you know and take it from there.

Awesome. Now we will take small steps, one by one to build this. Get your tools out soldier! We will need an Arduino, some connecting wires, 10 Kilo Ohm resistor, Push Button switch and an LDR.

Get the LEDs working

Let's brainstorm, what do we know about LEDs? We know how they work, we know there is an example on making LEDs blink, we know how we can use the LED on pin 13 to do quick checks if the board is working fine.

As a first step, let's get the LEDs working through the pin 13 using the LED blink example. You already know how to navigate to the example don't you my friend?

Here is how the code looks like right now:

```
// the setup function runs once when you press reset or power the board
void setup() {
  // initialize digital pin 13 as an output.
  pinMode(13, OUTPUT);
}

// the loop function runs over and over again forever
void loop() {
  digitalWrite(13, HIGH);   // turn the LED on (HIGH is the voltage level)
  delay(1000);              // wait for a second
  digitalWrite(13, LOW);    // turn the LED off by making the voltage LOW
  delay(1000);              // wait for a second
}
```

Code:

```
// the setup function runs once when you press reset or power the board
void setup(){
  // initialize digital pin 13 as an output.
  pinMode(13, OUTPUT);
}
// the loop function runs over and over again forever
void loop() {
  digitalWrite(13, HIGH); // turn the LED on (HIGH is the voltage level)
  delay(1000); // wait for a second
  digitalWrite(13, LOW); // turn the LED off by making the voltage LOW
  delay(1000); // wait for a second
}
```

Let's go ahead and upload this code on our board. I am using an Arduino Uno for this one. You know how to upload the program right? Refer back to `Chapter 1`, *The World around Us* if it slipped out of my mind. Come back here once you upload is done.

Keep checking out the console window (green/black window at the bottom of the IDE). If you see any form of errors, remember, we have learnt how to navigate ourselves in these situations. What do we do? Google it and figure out where the problem could have been.

Ok, we should have our LED on pin 13 blinking now. We will move on to the next step and test how would it look if we could control the blinking of the LEDs through an external influence. Let's use a switch to test this. We will press the switch and switch the LED on and off on the basis of the switch press.

 Curious about why we are doing this? Why a switch? Think about it and write it down in your notebook.

Testing an external influence on LEDs – pushbutton switch

We all know what a switch is don't we. We just read about it in the previous chapter. We know how it works conceptually. Let's see how it works practically and in circuits.

In this project, we will use a push button switch. This is how it looks.

Image source: https://www.sparkfun.com/products/97

The working principle of the switch is rather simple. You press it, circuit connection is formed hence the circuit works, if you release it, the circuit breaks, so the circuit doesn't work.

At the stage when the pushbutton is un-pressed, we will call the state of pushbutton to be open. When the pushbutton is pressed, we will call that state as closed.

We will use the following components:

- Resistor – 10KOhm
- Push button switch
- Breadboard

The following diagram explains how the circuit looks:

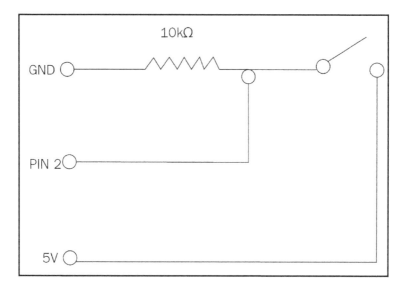

To make the above circuit connections, we are going to use a breadboard.

Do you know what a breadboard is? Find out what a breadboard is how it works using the internet. You could use:
https://learn.sparkfun.com/tutorials/how-to-use-a-breadboard to learn more about it. Return to this section once you have learned about the breadboard.

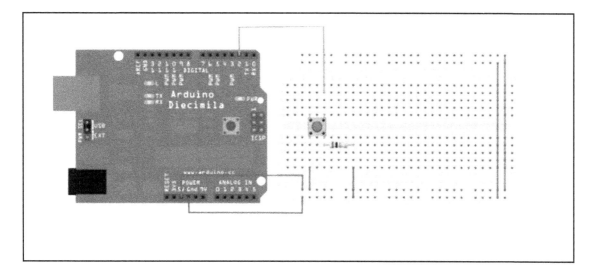

The above circuit shows the components in place. We will use the side rails on the extreme to run +5V in one line and GND on the other line.

We will proceed by connecting three wires to the board. The vertical rows will supply 5V and Ground. We will use Red wire and connect it to one of the vertical lines, this is the 5V line, black wire to the other vertical line. This will be our Ground line.

Digital pin 2 will be connected to one leg of the pushbutton using third wire, we will connect this to ground through a (10K Ohm) pull down resistor.

A pull down resistor brings any state which is not HIGH to LOW. More often than not, while working with switches, it was noticed that switches don't stay in the just open and closed state. There are times when the switch is released after pressing, but switch is neither completely open nor completely closed. This state is called a bouncing state. As the name suggest, switch is basically bouncing between states. So the pull down resistor is used to de-bounce the switch to a definite value of low.

The other leg of the button is connected to the 5 volts line. Let's look into details of what happens while the pushbutton is open or un-pressed. There is no connection between the two legs of the pushbutton, therefore the pin is connected to ground (remember we put the pull-down resistor?) and we read a LOW. Now, when the button is closed or pressed, it makes a connection between its two legs. This time, both the legs are connected to 5 volts, hence we read a HIGH.

If you disconnect the digital I/O pin from everything, the LED may blink erratically. This is because the input is *floating* – that is, it will randomly return either HIGH or LOW because the value is never absolute, it's like a balloon in a room that is neither touching the ceiling, not coming down to the ground. That's why you need a pull-up or pull-down resistor in the circuit.

Here is how the code looks like:

```
const int buttonPin = 2;      // the number of the pushbutton pin
const int ledPin =  13;       // the number of the LED pin

// variables will change:
int buttonState = 0;          // variable for reading the pushbutton status

void setup() {
  // initialize the LED pin as an output:
  pinMode(ledPin, OUTPUT);
  // initialize the pushbutton pin as an input:
  pinMode(buttonPin, INPUT);
}

void loop() {
  // read the state of the pushbutton value:
  buttonState = digitalRead(buttonPin);

  // check if the pushbutton is pressed.
  // if it is, the buttonState is HIGH:
  if (buttonState == HIGH) {
    // turn LED on:
    digitalWrite(ledPin, HIGH);
  } else {
    // turn LED off:
    digitalWrite(ledPin, LOW);
  }
}
```

Code:

```
const int buttonPin = 2; //the number of the pushbutton pin
const int ledPin = 13; //the number of the LED pin

//variables will change:
int buttonState = 0; //variable for reading the pushbutton status

void setup() {
  // initialize the LED pin as output:
  pinMode(ledPin,OUTPUT);
  //initaliize the pushbutton pin as an input
  pinMode(buttonPin,INPUT);
}

void loop() {
  // read the state of the pushbutton value:
  buttonState = digitalRead(buttonPin);
```

```
//check if the pushbutton is pressed
//if it is, the buttonState is HIGH:
if(buttonState == HIGH){
  //turn LED on:
  digitalWrite(ledPin,HIGH);
  }else{
    //turn LED off:
    digitalWrite(ledPin,LOW);
  }
}
```

On the press of the button now, the LED should turn on and off otherwise. We will save this code for now and move on. Remember, every problem is like a jig saw puzzle. We know this part of the puzzle is in the right place. We don't have to necessarily re-use this code, we just have to understand the concept here. Let's work on the other parts now.

Till now, we have got our LED working, and with a little bit improvement on the code, we have our LED working on the push of a button. Let me rephrase that. An external influence (button) is triggering an action (LED on/off). Now let's think about what we wanted our external influence to be. We wanted a light sensitive bot right?

The only part of the puzzle that is left now is to create light sensitivity. Let's work on that now.

Hi Computer, I'm Arduino! – Using serial communication to make your Arduino talk

The Arduino is no baby that just crawls around and blinks LED's. You can program it to speak!

We will see how to use the Arduino's Serial library to have the Arduino talk to the computer over the USB port.

Let's begin by making it clear that we aren't talking about tasty breakfast while talking about Serial. Serial communication is a type of "protocol" or a procedure by which information and data is sent one after another "bit by bit" instead of all at once. A bit is the fundamental building block of digital data, consisting of a 0 or a 1.

You need not to worry about the inner working of the protocol itself, but the end-result it can accomplish: Sending messages and data back and forth from the Arduino to a computer or even other hardware and Arduinos. Let us consider communicating between a computer and Arduino for now since we will be using it extensively in the book.

Let us understand Serial Communication Library by directly jumping into the code. Don't worry if you don't know what libraries are yet. You are correct, in guessing that we aren't talking about the libraries which have books and strict librarians with large spectacles.

Libraries will be explained in later chapters. For now, just think of a library as a collection of procedures or tasks that tell the Arduino to do certain things:

```
void setup()            // run once, when the sketch starts
{
   Serial.begin(9600);  // set up Serial library at 9600 bps
   Serial.println("Hello world!");  // prints hello
}
void loop()                          // run over and over again
{
                                     // do nothing!

}
```

Let us see the working of this code snippet:

```
void setup()
```

This part of the code, and everything between the { and } brackets runs exactly once when the Arduino runs.

The following procedure is part of the serial library, and tells the Arduino the speed at which communication should take place:

```
Serial.begin(9600);
```

The following table would give you an idea of how this line can be further broken up:

Library Name	.	Procedure Name	(Value)	;
Serial	.	begin	9600	;

This line of code says: begin the serial communication at the speed of 9600 bits per second (remember the 0's and 1's talked about earlier). This speed is sometimes called the "Baud Rate" of communication. The . Specifies that this procedure belongs to the Serial library.

```
Serial.println("Hello world!");
```

Similar to the previous command, the println procedure tells the Arduino to send data to the serial port. The data that will be sent is Hello World which is the value given to the println procedure. The following part of the code runs forever in a loop:

```
void loop()
```

We haven't put anything inside this because we want to send "Hello World" only once to the computer.

We now upload the code to our Arduino using the Arduino IDE. After uploading, we use the Arduino IDE's Serial Monitor to see what the Arduino is sending:

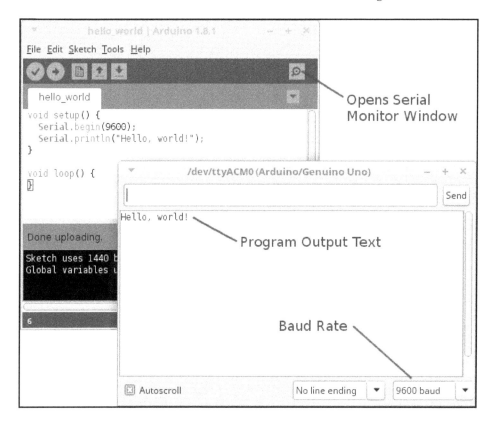

We make sure the baud rate in the Serial Monitor is set to the value we set on our Arduino. This is done so that our computer listens to the Arduino at the same rate at which the Arduino sends data, otherwise, the Serial Monitor will output gibberish.

You can see the the Arduino send "Hello World!". How exciting, your Arduino can talk now!

Try putting the Serial.println("Hello world!"); inside the void loop(){} instead of void setup(){} and see what happens.

We will be using the Arduino's serial monitor to output values of sensors to our computer so we have a better understanding of what's going. The Serial Monitor and Serial Communication are great ways to debug (meaning fix, in code-speak) sensors, connections and even code.

Light sensitivity sensor – LDR

We know how resistor works right? Let's go back to Chapter 3, *Components and Connections* for a quick recap and come back here. It essentially restricts the flow of electrons in a circuit. Light Depended Resistor is a special kind of resistor that reduces its resistance when light falls on it. How does that work you ask? Good question.

Let's dig a little deeper into what is LDR and how it works. First of all, this is how the symbol of LDR looks like:

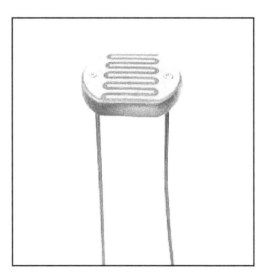

(Image source: https://cdn.instructables.com/F1H/DRCQ/IDCXJLG6/F1HDRCQIDCXJLG6.MEDIUM.jpg)

Symbol:

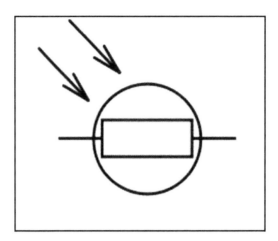

The arrow signs coming down show the light falling on the LDR. You know what everything in the world is made up of right? Remember we learnt about electrons in the beginning of the book? Electrons are the fundamental part of any material.

Let's start from there. So similar to electrons, photons are fundamental part of light. Light is not made up of only particles though, it has waves too (I know right? We think we know about science one day and the other day we don't! Exciting isn't it?). Learning more about the dual nature of light is out of the scope of this book, but I encourage you to use your googling skills to find out more!

Coming back to photons, they are the smallest part of light. Every photon has a lot of energy in it. So when they hit anything or any material they transfer a part of that energy to that material. Recall how we studied about a resistor slowing down the movement of electrons. Look at the following two diagrams:

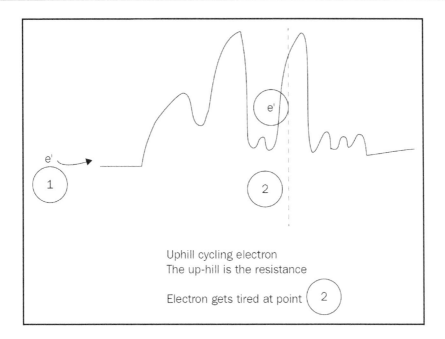

Uphill cycling electron
The up-hill is the resistance

Electron gets tired at point 2

The electron starts cycling at point 1 and gets tired at point 2.

An electron trying to cycle on a up-hill track. Its very difficult isn't it?

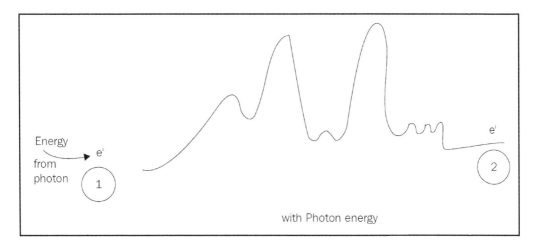

Energy from photon

with Photon energy

Electron now also has energy from the photon.

Now imagine if a friend starts pushing it from the back, it get additional energy, wouldn't it be much easier for it to go up hill now? This is exactly it works inside the LDR. Photons give more energy to the electrons to pass through.

So, in summary of the LDR, we know when light falls on the LDR, it will reduce the resistance of the LDR, electrons flow to the other part, hence the circuit is closed. OK enough theory! Let's get back to building.

 Find out how the screen in laptops and phones adjust their lights automatically. What kind of sensors do they use?

We will build another block of the jigsaw puzzle now. We will first test how the LDR works with an Arduino. Once we have successfully done that, we will think about integrating it with above piece. Remember LDR is going to be the final version of our external influence.

Following is the figure representing circuit connections:

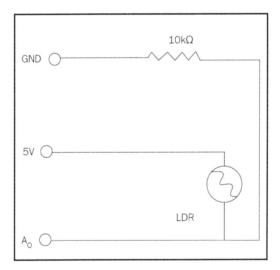

On connecting all the components, this is how the circuit will look like:

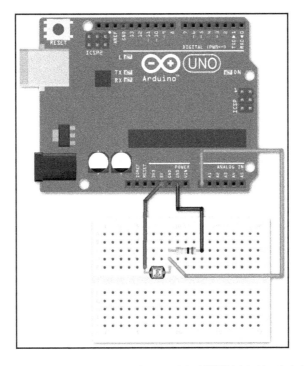

(Image source: http://www.tweaking4all.com/wp-content/uploads/2015/11/arduino-ldr-analog.jpg)

From the above diagram you can see that our LDR is connected to **A0** to give us an analog input. We will work on top of the analog read example from this example. This is how the code is going to look like:

```
int lightPin = A0;   //define a pin for Photo resistor

void setup()
{
    Serial.begin(9600);   //Begin serial communcation

}

void loop()
{
    Serial.println(analogRead(lightPin)); //Write the value of the photoresistor to the serial monitor.
    delay(10); //short delay for faster response to light.
}
```

Code:

```
int lightPin = A0; //define a pin for Photo resistor
void setup()
{
    Serial.begin(9600); //Begin serial communcation
}
void loop()
{
    Serial.println(analogRead(lightPin)); //Write the value of the
photoresistor to the serial monitor.
    delay(10); //short delay for faster response to light.
}
```

In the above code we will use the Serial Monitor to read the values. You will see after uploading the values, the serial monitor will start showing values anywhere between 0 to 1023. We however now know how to read the values from LDR.

Let's go back to the first two pieces of puzzle again.

We made a circuit that blinks an LED–from here we keep the code of turning LED on or off.

We made a circuit that uses a switch which when pressed switches on the LED. – We will keep the logic from here. This means that on certain level on input, I will switch on the LED (push button closed) and switch it off of another level (push button open). Our LED right now works with two states then, On and Off.

From the LDR experiment, we are going to do something very small, yet very important. We are going to define our own set of values on which the LED will be On and other set of values where the LED will be off. You saw that the LDR input is between the number 0 and 1023. Depending on your circuit, the numbers could not go down to 0 or reach 1023, but they will typically be in the range.

So how about this, let's try to see when do we get what numbers from the LDR? Run the code and cover the LDR with a small cloth or with just a thick paper. Do the Serial Monitor values go down or Up? Now remove the cover and read the values again. What do you see? Do you see a pattern?

In my case, when I cover the LDR, the reading becomes low in my case I get values under 800. When I remove the cover, reading becomes high. So let's look at the numbers. If the readings from the LDR were to be lower than 800, it means that LDR senses Darkness. Otherwise LDR senses Light. Let's work using these numbers and turn ON the LED when LDR senses darkness and OFF when the LDR senses light.

We will tweak the code we wrote for sensing LDR to the following:

```
int lightPin = A0;   //define a pin for Photo resistor
int ledPin = 13; // We are using inbuilt LED

void setup()
{
    Serial.begin(9600);   //Begin serial communcation
    pinMode(ledPin, OUTPUT); // Configuring pin 13 as output

}

void loop()
{
    Serial.println(analogRead(lightPin)); //Write the value of the photoresistor to the serial monitor.
    if (analogRead(lightPin) < 800){    //Darkness Detected by the LDR
      digitalWrite(ledPin,HIGH);

      }
    else {                               // When Light detected outside

      digitalWrite(ledPin,LOW);

      }

    delay(10); //short delay for faster response to light.
}
```

Code:

```
int lightPin = A0; //define a pin for Photo resistor
int ledPin = 13; // We are using the inbuilt LED

void setup() {
  Serial.begin(9600); //Begin serial communication
  pinMode(ledPin, OUTPUT); //Configure the pin 13 as output
}

void loop() {
  Serial.println(analogRead(lightPin)); //Write the value of the
photoresistor to the serial monitor.
  if (analogRead(lightPin)<800){ //Darkness Detected by the LDR
    digitalWrite(ledPin,HIGH);
    }
    else{                               //When Light detected outside
      digitalWrite(ledPin,LOW);
      }
```

```
    delay(10); //short delay for faster response to light.
  }
```

When all is done, compile the code, upload and check. If you notice that in your case, on covering the LDR you get another set of values, like 600 or less, keep the threshold according to that. Threshold is a bar that is set as a condition. If the new values from the sensor are lower than that bar (threshold) we perform one type of actions, if the input values are higher, we perform another set of actions.

Now that we have successfully done all the integrations let's reflect on what we have accomplished now. We have successfully created the brain of a bot that will switch on the LED when there is dark outside and switch off the LED when it is bright outside.

 Think of where else can you use this logic to build? Can you use this logic to switch off the lights in your room when you are not around? What sensor could you use for that? Maybe a motion sensor? Write down all the problems you would want to solve using this logic.

Now that we have successfully built the bot. Let me tell you the scope of what you have just achieved. No matter what sensor there is out there, it will work on the same logic. You will have an analog input, you will read the values using serial monitor and check what changes you see in different conditions. You will then set a threshold and on the basis of that threshold, you will perform actions. Look at the diagram below, it explains this a little better.

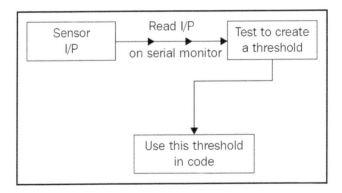

This is the process of using any sensor. Once you have figured out what thresholds to use, rest is simple!

Summary

We learnt a lot of very important things in this chapter. We integrated all the learnings from the previous chapters and finally built something smart. We built a brain! Just give a moment to let that sink in. You just created a smart organism, all by yourself. You are a creator now. And remember this feeling you have inside you. Never let this go. This is exactly how the inventors, astronauts, scientists and people who change the world feel.

From the next chapter onwards, we will dive deeper into building things. Don't let the excitement fade away.

6
Safety Box

Things you will learn about in this chapter are as follows:

- More Arduino input and output
- Making sounds
- Conditional operation in your code

Don't touch my stuff!

Do you have precious and important things that you would want to protect against the curious clutches of your siblings or friends?

Would you like to know if someone is meddling with your stuff?

If the answer to the above questions was *Yes!*, this next project is perfect to safeguard your things against people you don't want fiddling with your stuff.

We are going to build a safe, similar to the one you might have seen in banks, but yours is going to be special because it has an Arduino inside!

What you will need

- An Arduino Uno
- A breadboard
- Male to male jumper cables
- A Piezo buzzer
- 9V battery
- 9V battery clip
- Craft materials:
    - Scissor
    - Cardboard box
    - Aluminum foil
    - Cellophane tape
    - Glue

Let's get to work!

As you start working on more complex projects, it's a good idea to have a high-level understanding of what we are trying to achieve with what we are making and, subsequently, break it down into sizable modules that you can work on.

This would start with the *Problem Statement* or *Problem Definition* that outlines the problem that we are going to solve.

This would be followed with the *Solution*, which gives a brief outline of the functionality required to solve the problem.

Let's have a look at these concepts with respect to our project.

Problem statement: Unauthorized people are messing with your things.

Solution: Build a safe, which can be opened with a key. In case the safe is opened without a key, an alarm goes off, which will alert you of the intruder!

Simple enough, isn't it?

Let's break this solution of ours into blocks so that we can visualize this project more clearly:

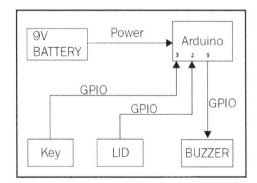

In the preceding diagram, you can see all the different parts of the project that work together to solve the problem statement.

Let's also define how these different blocks are going to work together.

The way in which our safe will work is as follows:

- If someone opens the safe without a key being inserted into the keyhole in the box, an alarm will go off
- If someone places a key in the keyhole and then opens the box, the alarm doesn't go off

Let's put this into a diagram that will define the flow in which actions would take place:

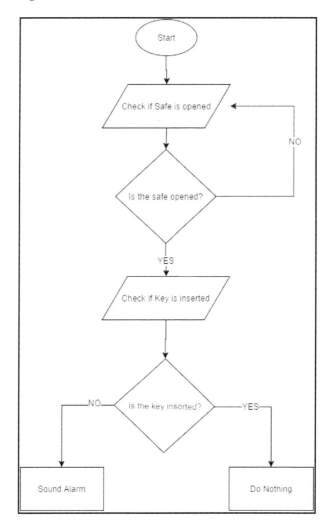

You can imagine the preceding diagram as if this is what the Arduino is thinking.

This diagram is also referred to as a *Flow Chart* since it describes the flow in which your project and, in turn, the code that you will put into the Arduino will work.

The *Start* defines where to start from. After this, there is a series and some tasks that are performed and decisions taken. We shall look at these one by one.

After *Start*, the Arduino checks whether the box is open or not. If the box is not open, the Arduino checks it again and continues checking until the box is opened. This is why there is an arrow pointing to the previous step. Doing this kind of task is also called a *Loop*. Hence, we say that we are checking whether the box in opened in a loop.

Only if the box is open does Arduino move on and get out of this loop and check whether there a key present in the keyhole.

If a key is present, the Arduino doesn't do anything and, thus, knows that an authorized person with a key has opened the box. But if the key isn't inserted when the box is opened, an alarm will be sounded.

Now, before we go on and start building things, there are a few more things left to understand. Bear with me, my friend, we are almost there.

I/O pins

As we mentioned earlier, Arduino has input and output pins along the edges of the board. These are also called I/O pins, in short. These pins form the physical interface between the Arduino and the outside world:

On the most basic level, you can think of them as switches that you can turn on or off (input) or that the Arduino can turn on or off (output).

These pins enable the Arduino to control and observe the outside world using electronic circuits connected to it. The Arduino is able to control LEDs by turning them on or off, run motors, sound sirens (now we're talking!), and perform many more such actions by giving an output signal on these pins. It can also detect whether a switch has been pressed, observe temperature or light levels by taking input signals.

Some of these pins have even more special functionalities giving the Arduino the ability to talk to other Arduinos or connect to the Internet or bluetooth using additional pieces of electronics usually referred to as peripherals. We won't be covering these in this book, but I do hope you go on to learn about them later and make amazing projects.

It's all about the logic

You may be wondering what it is with on and off, and how this translates into physical parameters or electrical signals. These will soon become clear.

We live in a world of analog signals–a countless number of colors that the eyes can see, a countless number of sounds we can hear, and a countless number of smells, and so on.

But with digital electronics, such as Arduino, we deal with discrete or distinct sets of values.

Logic levels, in a nutshell, describe the state that a signal is in. In digital electronics, such as Arduino, there are two logic states: 0 and 1. Since there are only two states, it is also called binary logic. This is also commonly translated to ON or HIGH for binary 1 and OFF or LOW for binary 0.

For Arduino, a HIGH signal is 5V, and LOW is 0V. This is how these logic levels manifest themselves physically in terms of voltage.

The Arduino uses these logic levels on its I/O pins to either take input from the outside world or give an output.

We shall see how these logic levels affect our project as we go further to understand the input and output devices that we shall be using in our project.

This is key!

Our Arduino will need to know or sense if a key is placed into the keyhole. This is an input that will be given on one of the Arduinos I/O pins.

Arduino can take an input from the outside world using the `digitalRead()` function.

A function in programming can be thought of as a task or a group of tasks that performs or does something. There are functions to add two numbers, there are functions that can check the number of letters in a word, and there are many more. You can even write your own functions in a program.

The `digitalRead()` function is one such function that gets input from the outside world through one of Arduinos I/O pins.

You will also be introduced to conditional statements, namely the *if* and *else* statements, which help the Arduino make decisions depending on certain conditions.

Let's write a program that takes input from a button, and depending on whether the button is pressed or not, turns on and off an LED. You learned how to blink an LED in the previous chapter using the `digitalWrite()` function. Using what you learned, we shall hook up a new circuit to our breadboard and see how digital input on the I/O pins as well as conditional statements work:

```
//Initializing a variable to store the value of the button state
int state = 0;

// the setup function runs once when you press reset or power the board
void setup() {
  // initialize digital I/O pins
  pinMode(2, INPUT);
  pinMode(13, OUTPUT);
}

// the loop function runs over and over again forever
void loop() {

  state = digitalRead(2);
  if ( state == HIGH )
    digitalWrite(13, HIGH);
  else
    digitalWrite(13, LOW);
}
```

Connect a button to the Arduino as follows:

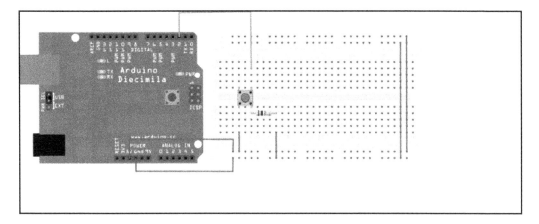

The equivalent connections will be like this:

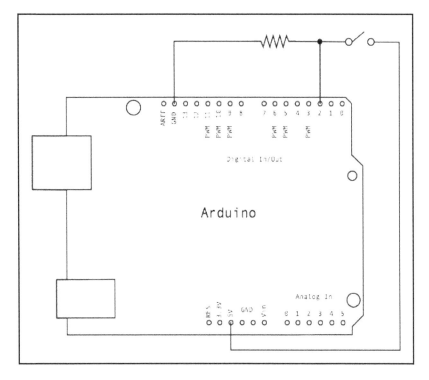

Image source: https://www.arduino.cc/en/Tutorial/Button

The working

When the button isn't pressed, there is no connection between the two legs of the button; it will input 0V to the Arduino since the pin of the button is connected to ground through the pull-down resistor. If you recall what we learned about logic states, the Arduino should read a `LOW` or binary 0 in this case.

Then the button is pressed and the connection is closed; this makes a connection between its two legs, thus connecting 5V to the Arduino's I/O pin, and we read a HIGH or binary 1.

Let's walk through this code, line by line, so that you can understand what each line does:

```
int state = 0;
```

This initializes a variable of an integer type and puts the value of 0 in it.

This is also called initializing a variable. In our case, this variable shall store the value of the state of our button. Values are assigned to variables using = ; hence, this is also called an assignment operator:

```
void setup() {
  // initialize digital I/O pins
  pinMode(2, INPUT);
  pinMode(13, OUTPUT);
}
```

In the `setup` function of Arduino, we use the `pinMode()` function to tell the Arduino whether we are using the I/O pins for input or output.

You will notice that there are some values inside the brackets of the `pinMode` function. These values are also called function parameters; they tell the function certain information so that it may work properly. In our case, for example, pinMode (2, INPUT) is telling the Arduino to set the I/O pin number 2 as an input.

Similarly, we have also initialized pin number 13 to be an output. There is an LED connected to pin 13 onboard the Arduino:

```
state = digitalRead(2);
```

In this line, we use the `digitalRead()` function to take the input from pin 2, which is the parameter that the function takes. It stores what it reads in the variable *state* that we defined earlier:

```
if ( state == HIGH )
    digitalWrite(13, HIGH);
  else
    digitalWrite(13, LOW);
```

This is where things get interesting. The preceding code snippet is allowing the Arduino to make a decision.

It stars with the if statement, which checks whether a particular statement is true or not. In this case, `if (state == HIGH)` is checking whether the value stored in the variable has `HIGH` in it.

Notice the double equals to sign? This shouldn't be confused with the assignment operator we looked at earlier. The `==` is a relational operator because it describes a relationship between two things.

If, the *if* statement is true, that is, in our case, *state* does store `HIGH`, it executes the command (or set of commands) following it, and thus the Arduino will write `HIGH` to pin number 13 using the `digitalWrite()` function, which takes the pin number and logic to write as its function parameters.

In case the if statement isn't true, the commands following the else statement is executed; thus, the Arduino will output a LOW signal on pin number 13.

Conclusion

When the button is pressed, the LED on the Arduino lights up, and when its released, the light goes out.

Make some noise!

Congratulations! You now have the basic concepts needed to get our safe working! There is only one thing left to do: to figure out how to output sound for an alarm.

We are going to use an output sound using a device called a buzzer:

Image source: https://www.robomart.com/image/cache/catalog/RM0338/piezo-buzzer-b-10n-piezo-electric-buzzers-rm0338-by-robomart-399-500×500.jpg

A buzzer is a two-terminal device, meaning it has to have two connections going up to it. This buzzer also has polarity, meaning it should be connected with one particular terminal of the two connected to 5V or `HIGH`, and the other connected to ground or `LOW`.

Let's hook up a circuit and make some noise!

Connect the components to the breadboard as shown. Make sure the pin of the buzzer near the + sign of the buzzer goes into the I/O pin of the Arduino. This pin is usually the longer one of the two.

The other pin would be connected to the Arduinos ground:

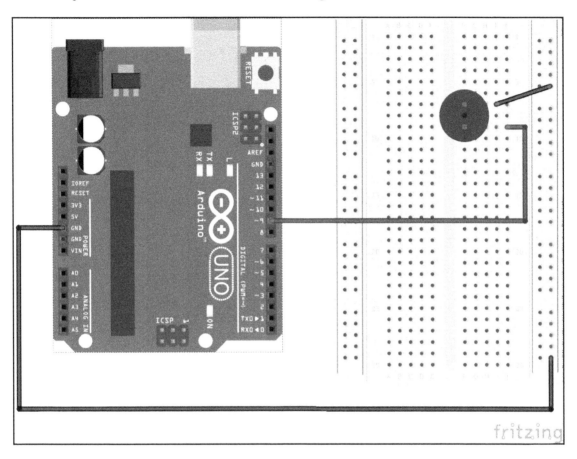

We shall now write a code that will bring the buzzer to life:

```
// the setup function runs once when you press reset or power the board
void setup() {
  // initialize digital pin 13 as an output.
  pinMode(9, OUTPUT);
}

// the loop function runs over and over again forever
void loop() {
  digitalWrite(9, HIGH);   // turn the LED on (HIGH is the voltage level)
  delay(1000);             // wait for a second
  digitalWrite(9, LOW);    // turn the LED off by making the voltage LOW
  delay(1000);             // wait for a second
}
```

There is nothing in this code that you don't already know from the previous chapter. We are going to use the code similar to the one you used to blink and LED to sound our buzzer, since the buzzer is also an output device.

Upload the code to your Arduino, and you will hear the buzzer go on and off.

The safe

You now have all the know-how to build our safety box!

Let's start with the code:

```
//Initializing a variable to store the value of the button state
int lidState = 0;
int keyState = 0;
int lidPin = 2;
int keyPin = 3;
int alarmPin = 9;

// the setup function runs once when you press reset or power the board


void setup() {
  // initialize digital I/O pins
  pinMode(lidPin, INPUT);
  pinMode(keyPin, INPUT);
  pinMode(alarmPin, OUTPUT);
}

// the loop function runs over and over again forever
void loop() {

  lidState = digitalRead(lidPin);
  if ( lidState == LOW )
  {
    keyState = digitalRead(keyPin);
    if ( keyState == HIGH )
      digitalWrite(alarmPin, LOW);
    else
      digitalWrite(alarmPin, HIGH);
  }
  else
    digitalWrite(alarmPin, LOW);
}
```

We start by storing the pin numbers in variables so that it doesn't become confusing.

We then initialize the pins to be either input o

In the `loop()` function, you can see that we r output. In the loop() function, you can see that we have used the conditional *if* and *else.* which will make the Arduino make decide what to do.

Also, notice that inside the *if* statement that checks whether the lid of the box is open or not, there is another *if* statement that checks whether a key is inserted.

When multiple commands need to be executed after an *if* statement, the commands are put in between curly brackets *{}* , as seen in the preceding code, after the Arduino checks whether the lid is opened or not.

Now that we have the code ready, let's get our hands dirty with the electronics and hardware to build the safe! You will be making your own switches that will detect whether the box is open, or whether the key is inserted.

We start by making a slot in our box in the size of our keycard in an appropriate place:

We take a piece of aluminum foil and place it on the keycard:

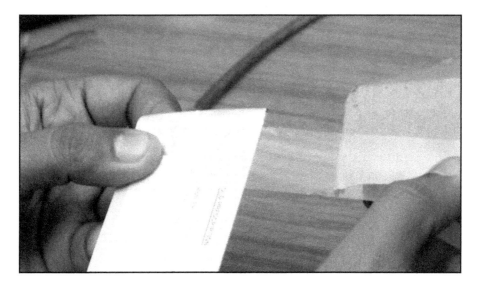

After cutting a male jumper wire, we strip the wire and tie it to a safety pin or a paperclip:

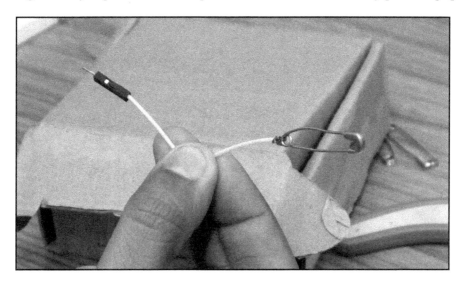

Make sure the wire is properly connected to the end so that it makes a good electrical connection.

The following image will give more clarity of the connections used in the model:

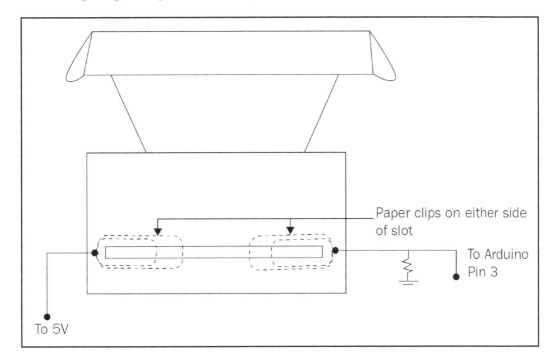

We glue-gun the safety pins to the inside of the box, such that they are exactly in the middle of the slot we earlier cut. The two safety pins we will glue need to be placed adjacent to each other with a small gap in between them:

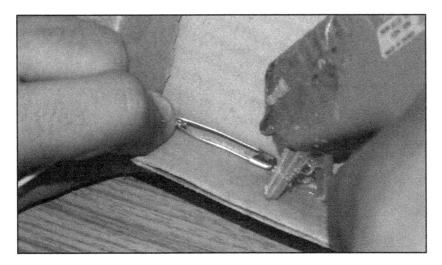

The following image will give more clarity of the connections used in the model:

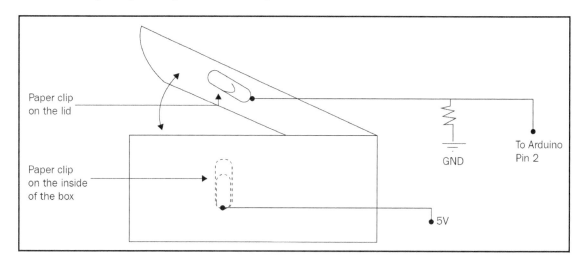

When the key card is placed in the slot, it will touch the two safety pins and complete the circuit similar to how a switch would work:

We do the same for the lid, placing one safety pin on the inside and another on the lid, such that when the lid is closed, a connection is made and the circuit would be complete:

Hook up the wires coming from the safety pins to your circuit with the wire from one safety pin going into the 5V output of the Arduino, and the other into the Arduino's digital pin:

Finally, the complete connection looks like as follows:

Summary

We were introduced to a whole bunch of new things in this chapter. Let's recap what we learned:

- We created a problem statement for our project, which outlines the problem we are going to solve
- We learnt how to make a flow chart, which describes the flow of how our code and project will work
- We learned about Arduino's I/O pins , which take input from the outside world and hence sense its surroundings using sensors, and also give output, which can control things such as motors, buzzers, lights, and so on

- We learned about logic levels and how they describe the state a signal is in
- We did a great deal of code and learned about various tools that help the Arduino think:
    - The assignment operator = that gives a value to a variable
    - How to use functions and pass function parameters to the functions that allow them to work properly
    - We looked at the *If* condition that helps the Arduino make decisions depending on relational operators, one of which is ==, which compares to see whether two variables have the same values stored in them
- We saw how we use the `digitalRead()` and `digitalWrite()` functions to read and write data to Arduinos I/O pins
- We learned how we can output audio through a buzzer and Arduinos I/O

7
Make a Friend

Things you will learn about in this chapter are as follows:

- More Arduino input and output
- Using a ultrasonic proximity sensor
- More conditional operations

Giving life to your toys

Ever wanted your toys come to life, like the movie Toy Story?

In this project, you will be doing just that, by using what we have learnt so far, along with new sensors that will enable the Arduino to see…

Well, sort of anyway.

Let's put together a problem statement for this project.

Problem Statement: Creating a toy that can come to life!

Solution: Create a robot that can sense the world around it using an Ultrasonic Proximity Sensor, and express its feelings using LED's.

Psst…come closer…

Before we move on to breaking this project into blocks, let's look at this new sensor that we are dealing with. As discussed earlier, a sensor is a device that gives an input to the Arduino, and tells it some kind of information about its surroundings.

An Ultrasonic Proximity Sensor, is a kind of sensor that gives the Arduino information about how close someone or something is to the sensor. It works by using very high frequency sound waves also called as ultrasonic waves, having frequency above 20,000 Hz. How this sensor can figure out the closeness of an object is similar to how bat's use their screeches to navigate while flying or hunting. You can visualize it by having a look at the following image:

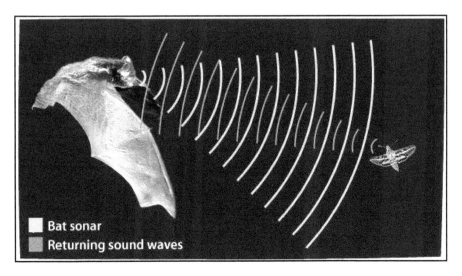

Image source: https://in.pinterest.com/pin/572731277582697045/

A bat emits a sound wave which travels through air and then bounces off of an object. The reflected sound or *echo* is then picked up by the bat's large ears.

Depending on how long it took for the sound to reflect back, the bat can then judge the distance of the object. If the object is far away, it takes more time for the sound to travel a larger distance, and will be heard by the bat later than when an object is closer.

 Ships also use a similar system for detecting objects underwater. Get the latest gossip about it from your friend, the internet.

Sensing the closeness in reality

How do we humans, sense this closeness in reality? Worry not, we have the Ultrasonic sensor to our rescue. Let's have a look at it in the following screenshot:

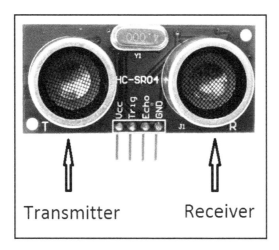

The sensor shown has a transmitter from which sound waves are emitted, and a receiver, that receives the reflected or echoed soundwaves.

The emitter and receiver are also called **transducers**. A transducer is a device that converts one form of energy into another. In this case, we are converting an electrical signal into soundwaves and vice-versa.

The Arduino starts by giving a HIGH signal to the `Trig` pin, which triggers the emitter of the sensor to emit a high frequency noise from one of its transducers.

After the sound wave is emitted, the Arduino waits for an input from the `Echo` pin. When the sound wave hits some object in front of it, it is reflected back towards the sensor, and is picked up by the receiver transducer, that then converts the received sound echo into electrical signal.

The Arduino then measure the time taken between when the sound was transmitted and the eco was received, and depending on how long this took, it will calculate the distance.

The Math to how this works is as follows:

We know that *Distance= (time x speed)*.

Since the distance actually covered by the sound wave is twice, that is, once from the origin to the object and then reflected from the object back towards the origin, the actual distance of the object would be:

Distance = (time x speed)/2.

Since it will be sound waves that will be travelling, that have a particular speed in air, *Distance= (time taken for reflected sound to travel x speed of sound in air)/2.*

Pictorial representation is shown in the following figure:

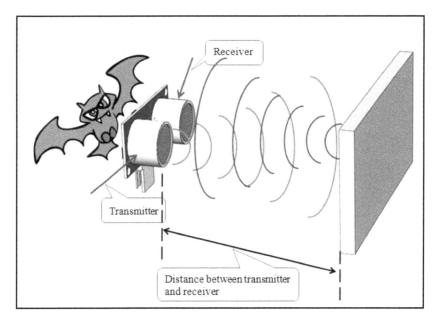

Image source: http://aimagin.com/blog/wp-content/uploads/2014/10/1.png

It's time now, to get our hands dirty! Let the Hunger games begin!

Let's get to work!

You know the drill, let's begin by making a High-Level block diagram of this project. It is shown in the following diagram:

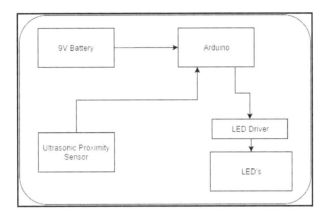

Let's now outline how this will all work together. When your toy senses someone in front of it, a smile made of LED's lights up, and when it doesn't sense anything, its LED smile goes away.

We will be using conditional statements again and the flow chart is as follows:

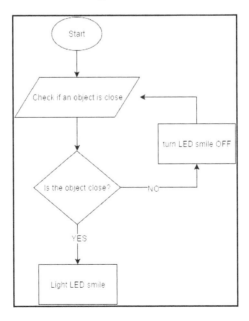

According to our flow chart, the sensor will constantly check if someone is close. If there is nothing in front of the sensor, the Arduino will make sure the LED's are off, and continue checking the proximity sensor. When an object is in front of the sensor, the LED's will light up.

Digging deep into Arduino libraries

We had discussed functions in the *The working* section of `Chapter 6`, *Safety Box*. If you would have thought that we will need to write our own function for getting the distance using our sensor, you would have been right, if it wasn't for, drum roll please....

Libraries!!

An Arduino library is a file that is a package of functions and declarations for other programs to use. Since we need to use the ultrasonic proximity sensor, instead of implementing the math ourselves, and writing our own functions, we can use the `<Ultrasonic Distance Library>`, which has the functions required to calculate and work with the distance sensor.

Downloading and installing an Arduino Library

To download and install the Arduino library, you must follow the following instructions:

1. For this project, you may download the library from:

   `http://playground.arduino.cc/Code/NewPing`

2. To install the library, put the `NewPing` folder in `libraries`.
3. In the Arduino IDE, create a new sketch (or open one) and select from the menu bar, Sktech | Import Library | NewPing.
4. You will notice `#include <NewPing.h>` gets added into your code.

Now that we have downloaded and installed the library, let's move on into the project.

Initializing the Library

Soon you will see how to use the functions that are included in the library, but before that you will need to initialize the library by using a *constructor* that provides the library with information so that it may work properly.

The following code snippet shows how to initialize the library, by creating an *object*:

```
NewPing distanceSensor(trigger_pin, echo_pin ) ;
```

Here we have created an object called `distanceSensor`, and passed information to it regarding which pins of the Arduino are being used for the **trig** and **echo** pin of the sensor as *parameters*. If we were using the pins 7 and 8 of the Arduino for the `Trig` and `Echo` pin respectively, the initialization would look like:

```
NewPing distanceSensor(7, 8 );
```

Understandably, this concept of constructors and objects may be confusing at first. Let me explain how this works by giving an analogy:

Imagine the *constructor* in our code to be a factory that builds cars. Now you can give the car that gets created a name, this is the *object* in our code. Now, we may need to tell the factory what car color we would like, and give this information to it, these are the *parameters* in our code.

We can even create multiple objects, if we want multiple sensors like:

```
NewPing Sensor1(7, 8 );
NewPing Sensor2(9, 10);
```

And so on.

Using library functions

Now that we have initialized our library, we can starts using functions and variables from it.

Let's go back to our car and factory example for a second. Now that we have our car built, we need it to do things, like drive around, close the doors etc. If our car was an object named `McQueen`, and had a function called `accelerate`, and `openDoor`, we can use as follows:

```
McQueen.accelerate();
```

And, we can use the other function as follows:

```
McQueen.openDoor();
```

If the function needs function parameters, like by what amount you want to accelerate, you can do that too:

```
McQueen.accelerate(100);
```

We have learnt how to use functions. Let us now get our hands dirty and dig deep to code for our sensor.

Getting familiar with the sensor

It's now time to write the code for the sensor. Let's output the values of the sensor to Arduinos Serial Monitor and play around with the sensor a little. We are going to use the `ping_cm()` function from the `NewPing` library. Other functions of the library are listed at `http://playground.arduino.cc/Code/NewPing`.

According to the web page the function is explained as follows:

`sonar.ping_cm();` Sends a ping, returns the distance in centimeters or 0 (zero) if no ping echo within set distance limit. There are other functions (also called Methods in some cases) that return the distance in inches, or the time it took for the eco to return, mentioned on the webpage.

Let's get coding for our sensor!

```
#include <NewPing.h>

NewPing sonar(8, 9);

void setup() {
 Serial.begin(115200);
}

void loop() {
  delay(50);
  int dist = sonar.ping_cm();
  Serial.print("Distance: ");
  Serial.print(dist);
  Serial.println("cm");
}
```

After connecting the sensor to the Arduino as shown in the following screenshot, and uploading you sketch, start your Arduino IDE's Serial Monitor to see a stream of information:

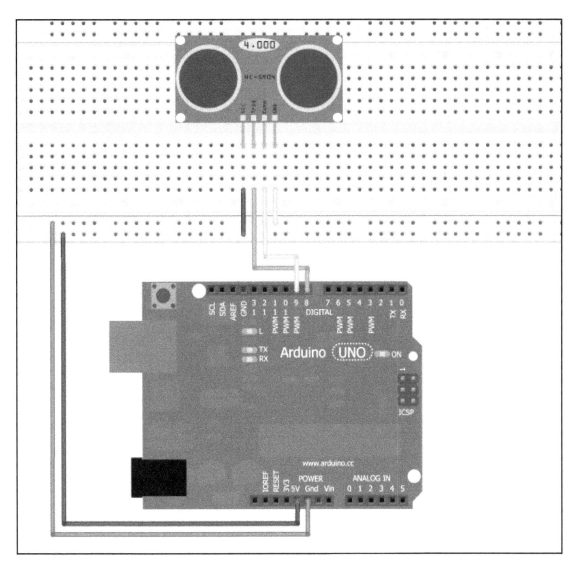

Image source: http://fritzing.org/media/fritzing-repo/projects/h/hc-sr04-project/images/HC-SR04-3.png

This is the stream of information from the sensor! Move your hand towards and away from the sensor and see the values change!

Now let's walk through this code:

```
#include <NewPing.h>
```

This includes the library in our sketch.

```
NewPing sonar(8, 9);
```

This initializes an object of the NewPing library and call it *sonar*, and tells it that the sensor's trigger pin, which is responsible to emit the ultrasonic wave is connected to pin 8, and the sensors echo pin, that gives an output when a reflected wave is detected is connected to pin 9.

```
void setup() {
  Serial.begin(115200);
}
```

Here we initialized the serial communication required for the Serial communication between the Arduino and the Arduinio IDE's Serial Monitor.

```
void loop() {
  delay(50);
```

We start our main loop by setting a time delay. The delay function halts the code for a specified amount of time in milliseconds as its parameter. This is required here because the main loop can cycle upto 16 000 000 times a second, which is VERY fast, and in our use case, unnecessary.

That is why, we introduce a small delay that stops the code for a small amount of time before proceeding. Here, we initialize an integer called dist that will hold the value of our distance read from the sensor We then assign it a value using the ping_cm() function we talked about earlier. Note how the function is used along with the sonar object we initialized earlier:

```
int dist = sonar.ping_cm();
```

Finally, we print the value to our Serial Monitor:

```
Serial.print("Distance: ");
Serial.print(dist);
Serial.println("cm");
}
```

Say hello to my little friend!

Now we have everything we need to know to start building our project. Let's start by writing the code:

```
#include <NewPing.h>
int ledPin=10;
int trigPin=8;
int echoPin=9;

NewPing sonar(trigPin, echoPin);

void setup() {

pinMode(ledPin,OUTPUT);

}

void loop() {
  delay(50);
  int dist = sonar.ping_cm();
  if (dist < 15)
digitalWrite(ledPin,HIGH);
    else
        digitalWrite(ledPin,LOW);
}
```

Like before, we start by storing the pin numbers in variables, so that it doesn't become confusing, and then initialize our LED pins for output. The code consists of a simple if statement that checks if an object is closer than 15cm, and if it is, lights up our LED's. If not, it turns our LED's off.

Now that our code is ready, let's build our project!

We begin by cutting out a head shape out of cardboard:

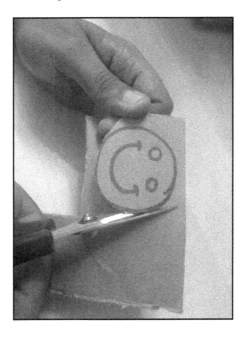

We pierce LED's through the eyes, that we have made on the face:

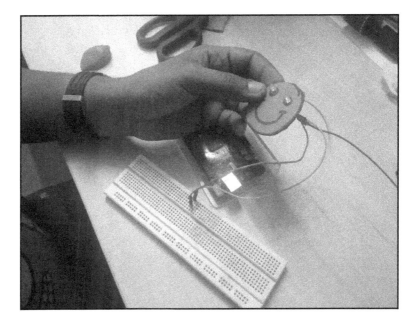

We connect the circuit according to the following diagram. Note that the LED's are placed in series, where the positive of one LED is connected to the negative of the other:

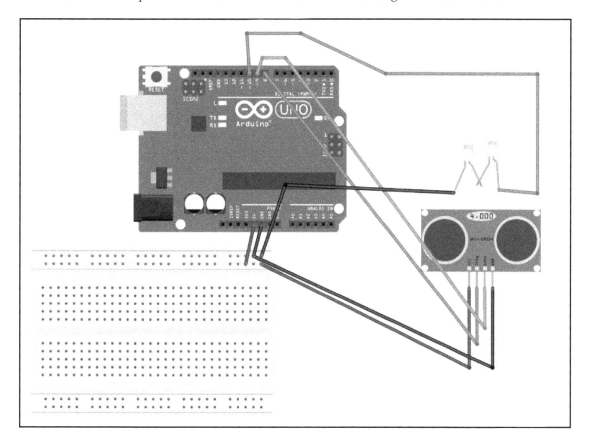

We also mount the head on a clay body we have made:

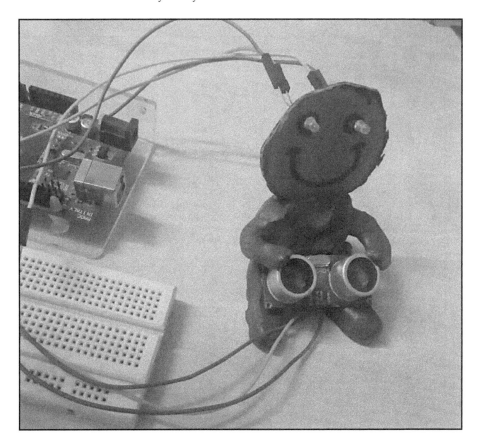

Connect and place the proximity sensor appropriately along with your new friend. If everything is connected properly, and the Arduino is powered up, when you bring your hand close to the Proximity sensor, the eyes should glow!

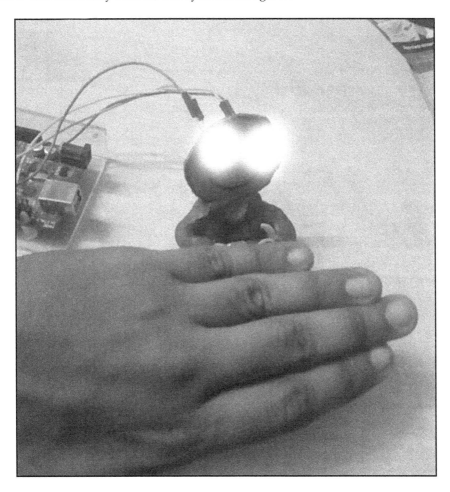

Summary

We explored many new things in this chapter, you need a pat on the back for getting through this!

Let's summarize what we learnt:

- How an Ultrasonic transducer works by measuring the time taken for sound to bounce off an object
- The math to calculate the distance would be:

    Distance= (time taken for reflected sound to travel x speed of sound in air)/2

- We revisited how conditional statements work
- We looked at how to add and initialize Arduino Libraries by using a `#Include` at the start of out code
- We saw how we use Library functions after initializing an object of that library, by using `objectName.functionName()`
- We finally used all that we learned and built our toy friend whose smile lights up when you approach it!

8
Save Energy

Things you will learn about in this chapter are as follows:

- Automation
- Using a light sensor

Automation? What's that?

You may have come across the word before, but what does it really mean?

According to the dictionary, automation is defined as:

The technique, method, or system of operating or controlling a process by highly automatic means

What this implies, is that a process or a device working by itself, with little or no human control is automation.

In this chapter, we will create a project that will help you understand this concept. We will be creating a *Smart lighting system*, which will turn on a light only when it is dark outside. Its smart, because it can do this without any human intervention, and hence is automatic!

Let's put together a problem statement for this project.

Problem Statement: Automating light depending on amount of ambient light.

Solution: A device that can sense the world around it using a light sensor, and depending on the amount of light, turn on, or off a light.

Detecting light

Let's look at the following new sensor that we are dealing with. We will be using a LDR, which stands for a Light Dependent Resistor. A LDR works on the principle of photo-conductivity An LDR is shown in the following figure to familiarize you with it:

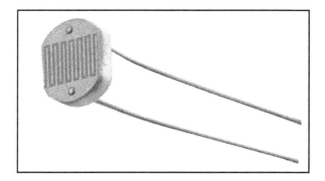

Image source : http://ninjagecko.co.uk/wp-content/uploads/2014/04/ldr.jpg

Photo conductivity is an optical phenomenon in which the material's conductivity (ability of the device to allow free flow of electrical charge) is increased when light is absorbed by the material.

 Remember, photo means light in Greek.

The surface of the LDR is made of this photo-conductive material. Typically, the resistance (apposition to the free flow of electrical charge) of the LDR is very high when there is no light falling on it. When light strikes the surface of the LDR, the resistance drops because of photo-conductivity and allows more current to flow across it as shown in the following representation:

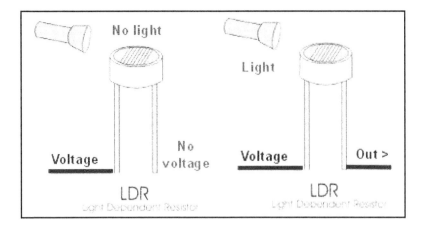

Image source: http://www.tnt-audio.com/jpg/ldrs.jpg

Also note that, the resistance of the LDR depends on the amount of light falling on it. The greater the amount of light, the lower the resistance, as shown in the following diagram:

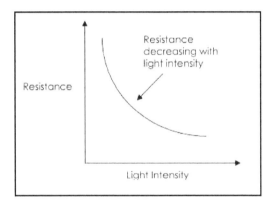

Image source : https://www.kitronik.co.uk/wp/wp-content/uploads/2015/03/how_a-light_depedant_resistor_works_resistance_v_light_intensity.jpg

Now that we know how the LDR works, shall we move ahead? Yes? That's the spirit!

Let's get to work!

Once again, let's begin by making a high-level block diagram of this project as shown in the following diagram:

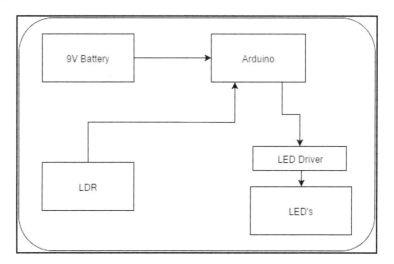

Let's now outline how this will all work together.

When our device senses that there is enough ambient or surrounding light, it will keep an attached LED off. But when then ambient light level goes below a certain threshold meaning the surroundings have gone dark, the device's light will turn on, more importantly, automatically!

We will be using conditional statements again and the flow chart is as follows:

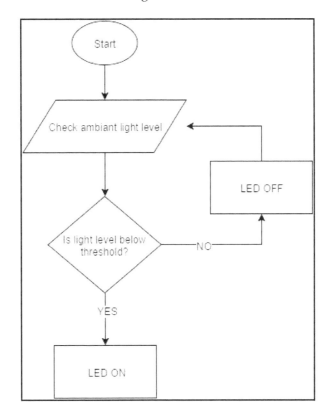

According to our flow chart, the sensor will constantly check the ambient light levels in a loop.

If there is enough light, the LED will stay off, but when the ambient light levels goes below a certain threshold, the LED will be turned ON.

Reading analog data

We mentioned earlier that the Arduino takes in digital data, which means that it can only handle numbers.

But what can we do for cases when we have an infinite number of possibilities, like light levels which cannot be quantified as a 0 or a 1, or ON and OFF?

Data like these which are continuous in nature, and do not have discrete or distinct levels are known as analog data. These signals in terms of voltage do not exist only at 0V or 5V, but vary between these two levels.

How do we go about reading such a continuous data then? Worry not, and remember, for all our problems, there's always a solution, we only need to think harder and explore.

ADC to the rescue!

An ADC, or an Analog-to-Digital converter is a circuit that converts voltages that are analog in nature to digital form.

The Arduino Uno has a 10 bit ADC inside it, which means it can convert an analog input voltage range, 0 to 5 volts, to a digital value between 0 and 1023 (2^10, hence 10-bit!).

The following table shows some analog voltages with their corresponding digital values:

Analog Voltage	Digital Reading
0V	0
1.25V	256
2.5V	512
3.75V	768
5V	1023

And the function that the ADC will employ is explained in the next section.

The analogRead() function

The `analogRead()` function of the Arduino is similar to the `digitalRead()` function we have been using, but is different in the respect that it uses the Arduinos ADC, and returns a value between 0-1023 instead of a HIGH or LOW.

The Arduino has pins marked **A0–A5.** These are the pins that are connected to Arduino's ADC, and can thus read analog voltages.

It's syntax for using this function is:

```
analogRead(pin)
```

Here `pin` is the analog pin between A0-A5 of the Arduino where the analog value will be given. Can you see where those pins are located in the following figure:

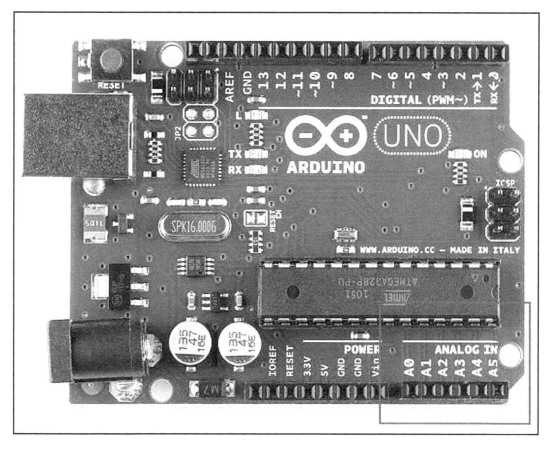

Arduino analog pins

Image source: https://cdn.sparkfun.com/assets/d/d/5/c/4/5114013ece395f527e000000.jpg

Let us see how to use this function by first interfacing our LDR and read its values to the serial monitor.

Wait, we need voltage!

Now, it may have become apparent after explaining how ADC's work, that the Arduino can measure only an analog voltage. But our LDR changes its resistance depending on the amount of light falling on it. So how can we effectively change the voltage across the Arduino depending on the change of the resistance of the LDR?

We use a voltage divider!

A voltage divider is a very fundamental and simple circuit which basically divides a larger voltage into a smaller one depending on the values of the resistors in its circuit.

A voltage divider uses two resistors in series with an input voltage and can output an output voltage that is a fraction of the input.

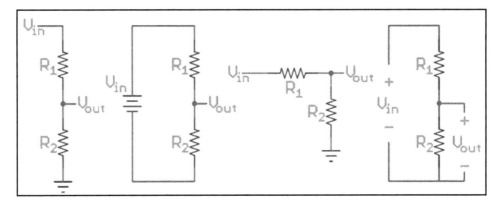

A voltage divider

Image source: https://cdn.sparkfun.com/r/600-600/assets/4/0/3/a/e/511948ffce395f7f47000000.png

The output voltage depends on the resistances and the input voltage by the following equation:

$$V_{out} = V_{in} \cdot \frac{R_2}{R_1 + R_2}$$

Now, using this circuit, along with our LDR, we can manipulate the voltage input into our Arduino. All we have to do, is keep one of the two resistors of the voltage divider a constant, and the other resistor will be our LDR as shown in the following figure. Depending on the amount of light falling on the LDR, its resistance will change, and in turn, will vary the voltage flowing into the Arduino. This change in voltage will allow us to figure out whether there is light falling on the LDR or not.

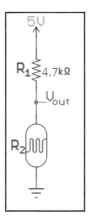

A voltage divider using a fixed resistor and a LDR

In this image, we have used a resistor of 4.5 kOhms because it is somewhere between the maximum and minimum resistance of the LDR. This is done so that we get a good variation in output voltages depending on the changing resistance of the LDR that follows the equation discussed earlier.

Now that we understand all there is to know to get our LDR to work, let's write a simple program to read voltage from an analog pin of our Arduino and output to the serial port.

Coding your way to light!

Let's cut straight to the chase!

Start by hooking up our circuit as shown in the following screenshot, you will need a fixed 4.7k Ohm resistor along with your LDR and Arduino to get it to work.

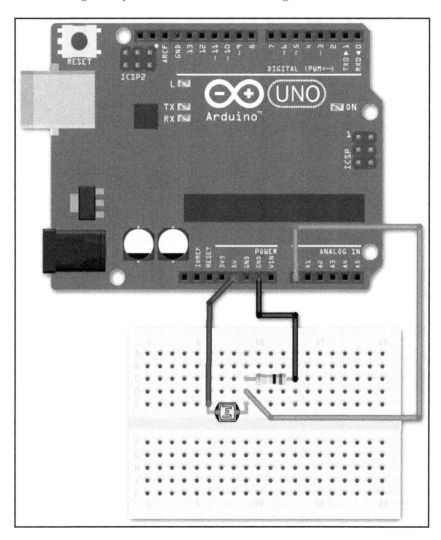

After connecting the sensor to the Arduino as shown, and uploading your sketch, start your Arduino IDE's Serial Monitor to see a stream of information.

```
int lightPin = A0;   //define a pin for Photo resistor

void setup()
{
    Serial.begin(9600);   //Begin serial communication
}

void loop()
{
    int level = analogRead(lightPin);
    Serial.println(level);   //Write the value of the photoresistor to the
serial monitor.
    delay(10); //short delay
}
```

After connecting the sensor to the Arduino as shown, and uploading your sketch using the Arduino IDE, start your Arduino IDE's Serial Monitor to see a stream of information.

This is the stream of information from the sensor! Cover the LDR with your hands preventing light falling on it and see how the values change. Shine a torch and see how it affects the values.

Now let's walkthrough this code. The following line initializes a variable that represents the Arduino pin we have connected our LDR to. Notice the A in front of the number, this corresponds to the analog pins on the left side of the Arduino:

```
int lightPin = A0
```

In the following code lines, we initialized the serial communication required for the serial communication between the Arduino and the Arduino IDE's Serial Monitor:

```
void setup() {
  Serial.begin(9600);
}
```

In the following line, we initialized an integer called level that will hold the value of the reading on the analog pin:

```
int level = analogRead(lightPin);
```

The following line prints the value stored in level:

```
Serial.println(level);
```

This was just a glimpse! Have you heard of the phrase, *there's always light at the end of the tunnel*? We'll see just that, there is!

Let there be light!

Now we have everything we need to know to start building our project, let's start by writing the code:

```
int sensorPin = A0;            // select the input pin for the ldr
unsigned int sensorValue = 0;  // variable to store the value coming from
the ldr

void setup()
{
  pinMode(13, OUTPUT);
  //Start Serial port
  Serial.begin(9600);          // start serial for output - for testing
}

void loop()
{
  // read the value from the ldr:
  sensorValue = analogRead(sensorPin);
  if(sensorValue<400)
      digitalWrite(13, HIGH);   // set the LED on
  else digitalWrite(13, LOW);   // set the LED off
}
```

We start by storing the pin numbers in variables, so that it doesn't become confusing, and then initialize our LED pins for output.

The code consists of a `if` statement that checks the value of `sensorValue`. If the values stored in it is less than `400`, meaning that the amount of light is less, it will turn the LED on, otherwise, it will turn the LED off. Note how we using another Relational Operator here, the lesser than < operator. Other relational operators include: Greater than (>) Greater or equal to (>=) Lesser or equal to (<=) Not equal to (!=).

Other relational operators include: Greater than (>) Greater or equal to (>=) Lesser or equal to (<=) Not equal to (!=)

Using these Relational operators and Conditional statements, the Arduino has the ability to make fairly advances decisions.

The threshold of 400 may be needing to change depending on the values you get. A good way is to check and determine the threshold using the Serial Monitor code we used earlier, and enter the value that the LDR gives when it's dark.

Hold on to your seats, the best part is yet to come!

The hut that comes to life at night!

Now that our code is ready, let's build our project. We use the circuit diagram as shown in the following screenshot:

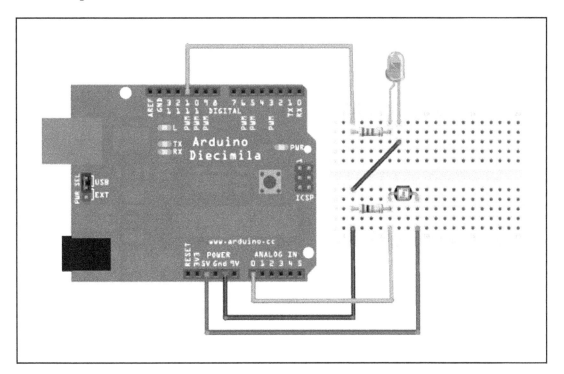

Once you have hooked up your circuit according to this diagram, it is time to take your automated lamp for a spin!

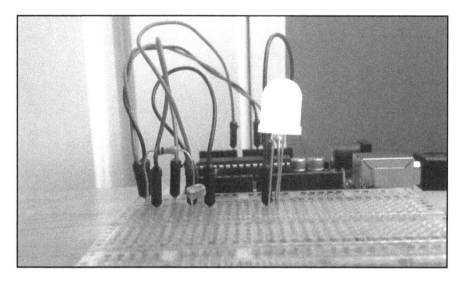

If you have set your threshold values right, you will find the LED to be OFF when there is ambient light present. Lower your threshold value in case the LED still remains on.

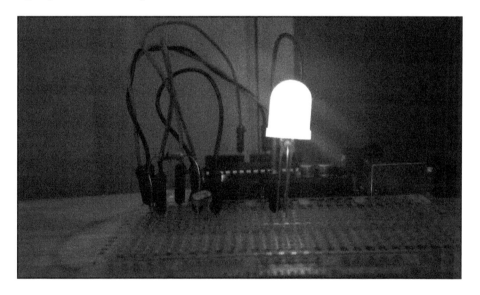

When your room goes dark, the LDR senses this change in ambient light levels and automatically turns your LED ON!

Summary

In this chapter we learnt:

- Automation is all about devices working on their own without human intervention. Smart street lights that turn on at night, Smart gardening systems that water plants are some examples of automation.
- Light Dependent Resistors and the phenomenon of photo-conductivity, where the conductivity of a material depends on the amount of light falling on it
- How to read Analog data on the analog pins of the Arduino using the `analogRead()` function
- The miracle of voltage dividers, and how they are used for converting a change in resistance to a change in voltage so that the Arduino can read it

9
High 5!

The topics that you will learn in this chapter are as follows:

- More Arduino libraries
- Interfacing a servo motor
- Making things move

You deserve a high 5!

You have come a long way and learnt a great deal of new concepts. You, my friend, deserve a high 5 for all that you have accomplished!

Since you are no ordinary person, you deserve not just any ordinary high 5, but one that the Arduino itself will give!

This brings us to our next new project, a High-5-ing Bot!

This project will use sensors that you have previously used, with new concepts of actuation using motors.

What you will need

Here's the list of components you will require for the project:

- An Arduino UNO A breadboard

- Male to male jumper cables
- An ultrasonic proximity sensor

- 9V battery
- 9V battery clip
- Servo motor
- Craft materials:
    - Scissors
    - Cardboard
    - A pen refill
    - Glue gun and glue

Motors and movement

Since we will need to make things move in this project, we will be using a kind of motor. A motor is a device that converts electrical energy into mechanical energy, in other words, one that converts electricity into motion.

Various types of motors

Image source: https://cdn-learn.adafruit.com/assets/assets/000/016/662/medium800/components_IMG_4846.jpg?1400434765

There are a vast number of motors out there… depending on the type of motion needed (linear or rotary), motor construction (brushed, brushless, stepper motor), type of current (AC or DC), and so on. Depending on what kind of motion we are looking for, which in turn depends on our application, we need to choose a motor that suits our requirements.

For our project, we will be using a **Servo Motor**, whose specialty is that it can move by specific amounts, or to a specific position, and even control its acceleration and velocity. Servo motors are traditionally used in RC cars and airplanes, but they can be used for all sorts of applications where precise control of position is required.

A servo motor

Image source: https://cdn.sparkfun.com//assets/parts/2/4/3/2/09065-01a.jpg

If you took an ordinary motor, one that you typically find inside toys, you will find that they have two wires coming from them. If you apply voltage to it, the motor will begin to spin in one direction, and when you reverse the voltage direction by interchanging the wires, you will find that the direction also reverses.

In contrast, a Servo Motor has three wires: Power, Ground, and a third wire for command input. As mentioned earlier, a servo motor will move to a specific position, which would be specified through its command pin.

A servo is able to achieve this because of **Feedback.** There is a sensor coupled with the physical output of the motor that measures its position and velocity. The servo also has an internal controller that makes sure that the position and velocity of the output match the parameters taken as input from the command pin.

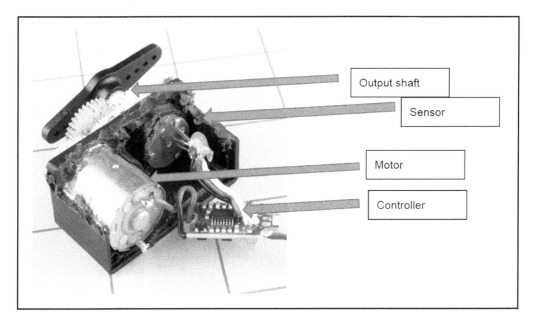

Internals of a servo motor

Image source: https://cdn.sparkfun.com/assets/learn_tutorials/5/2/6/servo-guts_1.jpg

Usually the hobby servos typically come with attachments for their shafts in the form of wheels or levers. These are called servo *horns*. These are useful when attaching the mechanisms that the servo will be driving to its shaft.

Servo Horns

Image source: http://www.spektrumrc.com/ProdInfo/SPM/450/SPMSP3000-450.jpg

Let's get to work!

You more or less have the building blocks ready for this project. Let us proceed with the rest of the project.

Problem Statement: Give yourself the robotic High-5 you deserve!

Solution: A High-5-ing robot that senses if your hand is close, and moves to High-5 you.

You have probably guessed it. We are going to use our good ol' ultrasonic proximity sensor to sense your hand.

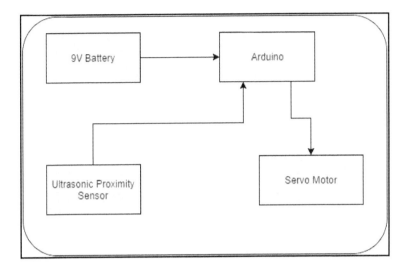

So, the way our robot will work is as follows:

- The proximity sensor is placed in front of the servo, whose shaft is connected to a cardboard cutout of a hand via a servo horn
- When you move your hand close to the servo, it will lift the hand to give you a High-5!

Let us put this into a diagram that will define its flow:

According to this flowchart, the proximity sensor will continuously check if an object (your hand) is close or not. When nothing is detected, the servomotor's position will keep the attached cardboard hand in the down position.

If it detects that your hand is close, the servo motor instantly lifts up its hand to give you a high-5!

The servo library

The servo library is one of the inbuilt Arduino libraries, meaning it comes part of the Arduino IDE and you don't have to download anything. Just initialize and use!

As you have learnt before, to add a library, you will need to go to **Sktech** | **Import Library** | **Servo** to include it in your sketch.

Notice all the other inbuilt libraries that are there. I hope one day you become an Arduino ninja and be able to use all of them, and possibly write your own libraries some day!

So, after you include the servo library, the `#include<Servo.h>` gets added to your code.

The servo library brings with it a set of useful functions that will enable you to use Servo motors properly. Some of these functions are:

- `attach()`: This function attaches a servo to a pin in the code. The following piece of code will attach a servo to a specified Arduino pin:

    ```
    myservo.attach(9)
    ```

- `write()`: This function writes a value to the servo, thus controlling the rotation of the output shaft of the servo, setting it to a specified angle in degrees. The following piece of code will rotate the shaft of the servo motor to 90 degrees from origin:

    ```
    myservo.write(90)
    ```

- `read()`: This function reads the current angle of the servo.

Getting familiar with the servo

Before getting onto our project, let's play around with some simple code that will get you familiarized with the servo library, as well as using a servo.

Image source: https://learn.sparkfun.com/tutorials/hobby-servo-tutorial

A note on the colors of these wires: different manufacturers of servos have different color-coded combinations of these wires. The following table will help you attach the servos to your Arduino:

Pin number	Signal name	Color scheme 1 (Futaba)	Color scheme 2 (JR)	Color scheme 3 (Hitec)
1	Ground	Black	Brown	Black
2	Power supply	Red	Red	Red or Brown
3	Control signal	White	Orange	Yellow or White

Connect the Servo to your Arduino in the following manner:

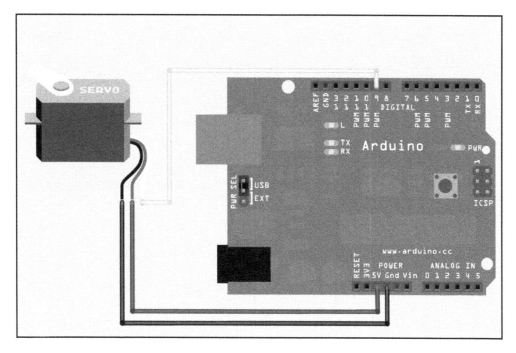

Image source: http://library.isr.ist.utl.pt/docs/roswiki/attachments/rosserial_arduino(2f)Tutorials(2f)Servo(20)Controller/arduino_servo.png

Now let's write some code that should get you used to using a servo:

```
#include <Servo.h>
Servo myservo;  // create servo object to control a servo
void setup()
{
  myservo.attach(9);  // attaches the servo on pin 9 to the servo object
}
void loop()
{
    myservo.write(0);
    delay(1000);
    myservo.write(90);
    delay(1000);

    myservo.write(180);
    delay(1000);

    myservo.write(90);
    delay(1000);
}
```

Understanding the code

Once the code is uploaded to the Arduino, the servo motor will cycle through different positions and come back to its initial position.

The following code includes the Servo library, and creates a Servo object called `myservo`:

```
#include <Servo.h>
Servo myservo;  // create servo object to control a servo
```

In the `setup` function of the Arduino, we attach the servo's command wire to pin 9 of the Arduino, as follows:

```
void setup()
{
  myservo.attach(9);  // attaches the servo on pin 9 to the servo object
}
```

In the following piece of code, we tell the servo to move to angle 0, following which we give a delay of 1 second to give the servo enough time to move to this position, before we tell it to go to other positions:

```
myservo.write(0);
delay(1000);
```

In the subsequent lines of code, we tell the Arduino to go to the 90 degree position, 180 degree position, and then back again.

High five!

Now you have everything you need to create your High-fiving robot!

We will use the ultrasonic proximity sensor we used in the previous chapter, along with conditional statements and relational operators to get everything working the way it should:

```
#include <NewPing.h>
#include <Servo.h>

NewPing sonar(2, 3);
Servo myservo;
void setup() {
myservo.attach(9);
}
void loop() {
  int dist = sonar.ping_cm();
  if (dist<15)
  {
    myservo.write(90);
    delay(1000);
  }
  else
  {
    myservo.write(0);
    delay(1000);
  }
}
```

We begin by including the necessary libraries, our ultrasonic library, and the Servo library and initialize objects: `sonar` and `myservo` respectively. We attach our ultrasonic sensor to pins 2 and 3 of our Arduino and the servo to pin 9.

We then read the value of our distance sensor. To check if your hand is close, use an `if` conditional statement along with a lesser than (<) relational operator. Thus, if an object is detected, the servo will rotate to the 90 degree position to give you a high five, or else remain at 0.

We start building our project by cutting a piece of cardboard shaped like a hand:

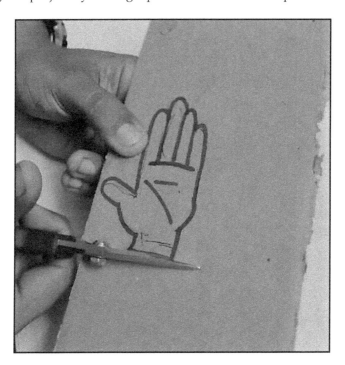

We use a BBQ stick or a pen refill as an arm for our hand. We glue one end of the pen refill to our servo horn and the other to the hand itself using a hot melt glue gun:

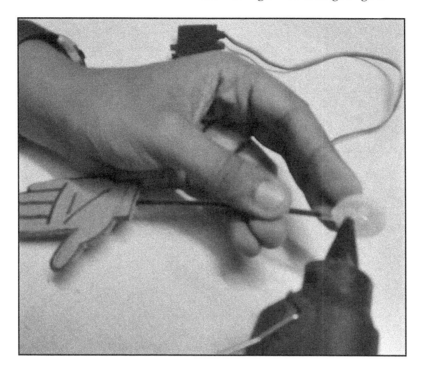

We make the necessary electronic connections using our breadboard to our servo and ultrasonic proximity sensor:

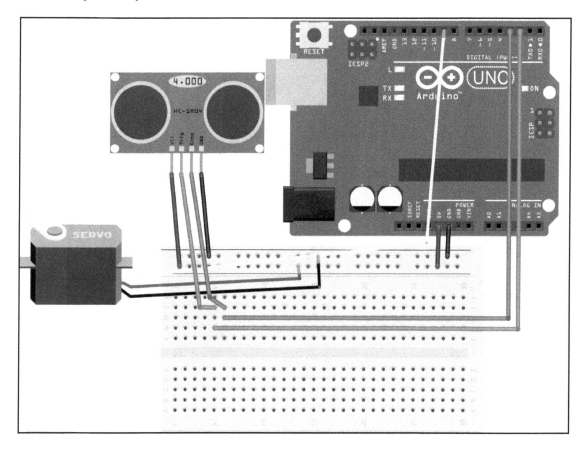

We glue the servo to the edge of a table using our glue gun. Place the ultrasonic proximity sensor in such a way that it can detect if your hand is close to the servo:

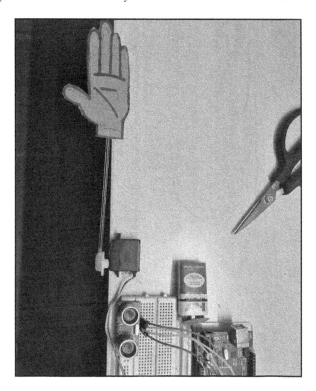

And, here you go:

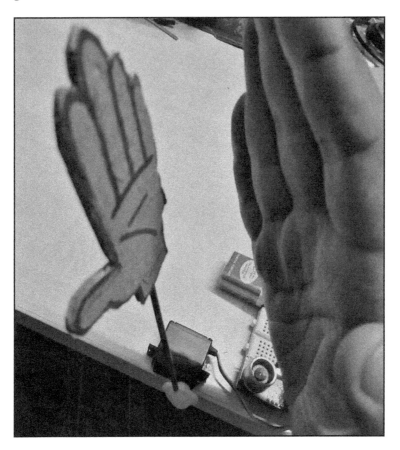

High five! You made it!

Summary

We were introduced to a whole bunch of new things in this chapter. Let's recap what we learned:

- Making things move!
- Different kinds of motors and how they need to be selected based on their application.
- The amazing servo motors whose exact position, speed, and acceleration can be controlled.
- Servo horns and attachments for different applications.
- The Servo library, along with a host of new functions!
- How to wire a servo to your Arduino.
- Giving yourself a high five!

You can use the concepts we learned here to make things such as automatic door locks or use the servo to press physical switches or turn knobs.

10
Plant, Meet Arduino!

The things you will learn in this chapter are as follows:

Creating your own sensor with stuff from around your house.

Making your plants talk

Caring for a plant can be a lot of responsibility. After all, they are living things, and you wouldn't want anything dying on your watch!

Gardening can be complex, making sure there is enough sunlight or your plant is getting enough water. Things can go wrong if care isn't taken while tending to your plants.

But you are no ordinary gardener, are you? You are going to use the magical power of the Arduino to bring gardening into the 21st century! We are going to be using the concept of automation as well as the sensors and circuitry we have used before to make our digitally empowered plant!

Problem Statement: Build a smart-gardening system.

Solution: A system that can quantify the amount of moisture in soil, and automatically intimate a human being if the plant needs to be watered.

What you will need

You will need the following things:

- An Arduino Uno
- A breadboard
- Male-to-male jumper cables
- Iron nails
- A buzzer
- A potted plant
- 9V battery
- 9V battery clip

I'm thirsty!

One of the biggest challenges we will be tackling in this project is to figure out if our plant needs to be watered or not.

We do this by measuring the moisture, or the water content of the soil that the plant is in. We will need to measure some quantifiable parameter that directly relates to the moisture of the soil.

This is where our sensor becomes important. As we have discussed before, a sensor is something that converts a physical parameter into an electrical signal that can be measured. In this case, the physical parameter is the soil moisture itself that we want to convert into electric signals.

Commercial soil moisture sensors estimate water content based on the dielectric constant of the soil. The dielectric constant can be thought of as the soil's ability to conduct electricity. The dielectric constant of soil increases as the water content of the soil increases.

This is due to the fact that the conductivity of water is much more than that of soil and its components. Almost 40% of soil is made of air pockets, whose conductivity is very small.When these air pocket get filled with water, it makes the soil more conductive.

Measuring the conductivity of soil

You can visualize the soil to be a kind of resistor, similar to the LDR we used earlier. The lesser the water content, the more the resistance; and the more the water content, the lesser the resistance.

Now, before we try and figure out what kind of circuit to use for our project, we need to find a way in which we can connect our wires to the soil!

We know that metals are good conductors of electricity. We need to provide a voltage between two points in the soil. We can use a large metal object, like an iron nail that can be embedded into the soil such that it can be an interface between our circuit and the soil.

Usually, these objects that are used as an interface in order to make some measurement are referred to as **probes**. You might have seen doctors using probes used to measure muscle activity of an athlete:

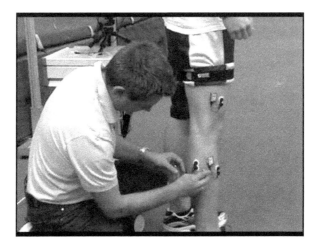

Image source: http://i.ytimg.com/vi/yZ_nxY91yxI/hqdefault.jpg

Muscle activity of an athlete being tracked using muscle probes.

The following is an image of a multi meter probe:

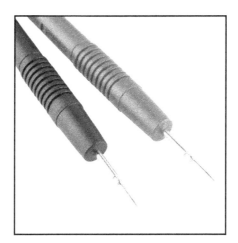

Example of multimeter probes

Now that we know we will be using some kind of probe to interface with the soil, let's proceed to see what kind of circuitry is required for it.

As mentioned before, the soil can be thought of as a resistor connected to the probes, like this:

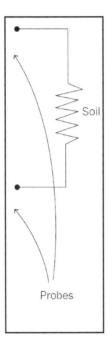

Since the resistance of the soil would be varying with the moisture of the soil, can you guess what circuit we will use to interface this with an Arduino? Depending on the change in resistance, we need to vary the amount of voltage across the Arduinos input pin.

If you thought of using a voltage divider, then go get yourself a High-5 from the bot in the previous chapter!

Just to recap, a voltage divider divides a larger voltage into a smaller one depending on the values of the resistors in its circuit.

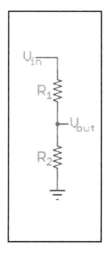

A voltage divider uses two resistors in series with an input voltage. The output voltage that is a fraction of the input. Thus, the equivalent circuit using a voltage divider would be:

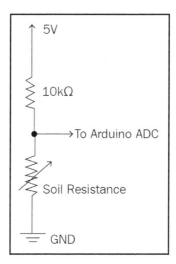

We use a resistor of 10K Ohms because it is somewhere between the minimum and maximum value of the resistance of soil. Thus, by the equation discussed in Chapter 8, *Save Energy*, this would output a wide range of voltages depending on the changes in the resistance we want to observe.

Let's get started!

Now that have all our building blocks in place, let us put it all together to create our cyber plant!

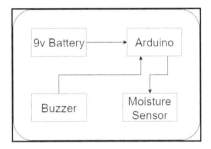

Let's now outline how this will all work together.

Our Arduino will continuously read the value of our moisture sensor via the **ADC** pin. We will be providing a threshold value for a particular amount of moisture. If the moisture sensor crosses this threshold, the buzzer will sound, alerting us that our plant needs to be watered.

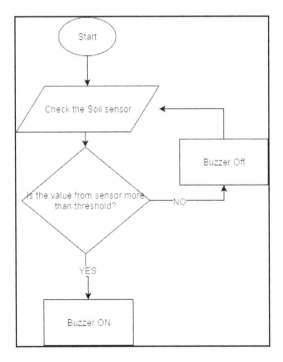

According to our flow chart, the sensor will constantly check the soil moisture sensor in a loop.

If there is moisture, the buzzer will not sound, but when the water moisture level goes below a certain threshold, the buzzer will sound an alarm.

Let's begin writing our code. As you have probably already figured out, we will be using the Arduino's ADC with the analog pins to read our moisture sensor using the `analogRead()` function, and output to our buzzer using the `digitalWrite()` function.

One thing that you should note is that according to our circuit, the soil moisture is inversely proportional to the voltage reading that we will get from the **Vout** pin of the circuit. This means that if the soil is drier, the voltage reading from our sensor will be higher than what we would get if the soil was moist.This is because of the way we have made our voltage divider.

We will accordingly create conditional statements that will create the basis for the logic according to which this project will function.

We begin by assigning names to the pins of the Arduino that we shall be using so as to reduce ambiguity in our code, in our `setup()` function:

```
int sensorPin = A0;
int buzzerPin = 6;
int threshold = 500;

void setup() {
pinMode(sensorPin, INPUT);
pinMode(buzzerPin, OUTPUT);
}
```

In our main `loop()` function, we begin by reading the value of our moisture sensor, following which we compare this value with a threshold we have set. Notice that when the reading of moisture is greater than the threshold, the buzzer will buzz, alerting that the plant needs to be watered. This is because an increase in the value of moisture means that the soil is becoming drier:

```
void loop() {
  int moisture = analogRead(sensorPin)
  if (moisture > threshold)
  {
    digitalWrite(buzzerPin, HIGH);
  }
  else
  {
    digitalWrite (buzzerPin, LOW);
```

```
    }
}
```

If the value of moisture is greater than threshold, meaning that our soil has become dry, we sound the alarm, and otherwise keep it off.

We start hooking up our circuitry as shown in the following schematic:

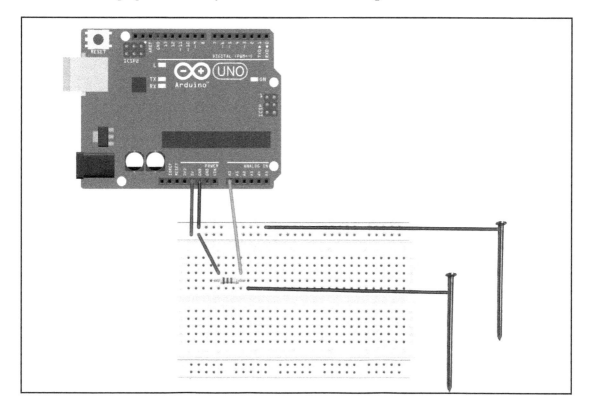

We connect wires to the two iron nails. Make sure that the wire makes good contact with the nails. Take an adult's help to solder these wires for best results:

Place the nails deep into the soil, about 1-2 cm apart. Make sure that they do not touch each other and there is only soil in between them:

Connect the other ends of the wires to the circuit you hooked up earlier.

Summary

This was a fun chapter to get you used to solving real-world problems. Think of ways in which this system can be improved by adding other sensors like an LDR or actuators like a water pump to make this project even better.

Let's recap what we learned:

- Understanding the dielectric constant of the soil, which can be thought of as the soil's ability to conduct electricity
- How we can interface the soil to our circuit using probes
- Then we came across our super voltage divider circuit again
- Using conditional statements to give our project logic

You have got through the journey in this book with flying colors, High-5! (Use the Bot!)

I hope what you have learnt so far would have changed your perspective of how you can do things by creating objects that can think for themselves and interact with you or the world around them.

This is just the beginning of the huge playground of sensors, actuators, electronics, and mechanisms out there that control everything from the automatic breaking system in cars to helping an airplane land safely.

Be inspired to use technology to solve real-world problems, and come up with innovative and efficient solutions at the same time. The world needs people like you!

Good luck, and may the force be with you!

Index

www.ingramcontent.com/pod-product-compliance
Lightning Source LLC
LaVergne TN
LVHW081340050326
832903LV00024B/1243